AMERICAN CRYPTIC

By Jim Towns

Anubis Press
Louisville, KY

Thank you for reading! If you like the book, please leave a review on Amazon and Goodreads. Reviews help authors and publishers spread the word!

To keep up with more Anubis Press news, join the Anubis Press Dynasty on Facebook.

ALSO BY JIM TOWNS:

SHORT FICTION:

"Warlock's Eye" – *One Night in Salem* (FunDead Publications, 2017)
"Special Service" – *Longshot Island Literary Magazine* (2017)
"Fools at the Feet of a Hanged Man" - Dodging the Rain literary magazine (2017)
"Castrato" – *Shades of Santa* (Things in the Wall, 2017)
"The Grave" - *The Devil's Hour* (Hellbound Books, 2019)
"Bad Coffee and the Bomb" - Switchblade Magazine (Caledonia Press, 2019).

NON-FICTION:

"The Attic Apartment" - *Paranormal Encounters* (Anubis Press, 2019)
"The Old Asylum" - *Handbook for the Dead* (Anubis Press, 2019)

FEATURE FILMS:

Prometheus Triumphant: a Fugue in the Key of Flesh
Stiff
House of Bad
State of Desolation

AMERICAN CRYPTIC

By Jim Towns

Copyright © 2020
All Rights Reserved

An Anubis Press publication
Anubis Press is an imprint of Frightening Floyds Publications

Edited by Jacob Floyd
Cover Photo and Design by Jim Towns
Illustrations by Jim Towns

No portion of this book may be copied or transmitted in any form, electronic or otherwise, without express written consent of the publisher or author.

This book is intended strictly for entertainment and is meant only to tell the stories of paranormal lore and various legends. Such tales cannot be individually confirmed or corroborated; the author and publisher make no claim to validate their accuracies.

AMERICAN CRYPTIC

BY JIM TOWNS

WITH ILLUSTRATIONS BY THE AUTHOR

For Martha, who liked old things.

CONTENTS:

INTRODUCTION

GHOST STORIES
1. THE LOPING SHADOW..01
2. THE ATTIC APARTMENT......................................06
3. STRANGERS ON THE TROLLEY............................14
4. MARKS OF A PITCHFORK....................................21
5. THE FALLING CHRISTMAS TREE...........................24
6. EFFIE..27

BOOGEYMEN
7. THE SIX-TOED MAN..31
8. THE PARK DEVILS..39
9. THE GREEN MAN...44
10. INDIAN PETER...52

UNCANNY PLACES
11. THE DEER CORPSE GOD....................................60
12. THE OLD ASYLUM..64
13. THE GIANTS UNDER THE MOUNDS.......................70

AFTERWORD...80

ABOUT THE AUTHOR
BIBLIOGRAPHY
ALSO FROM FRIGHTENING FLOYDS PUBLISHING
COMING SOON

INTRODUCTION:

"History is an inventory of ghosts."
-Guillermo Del Toro

The Author (age 10) at the grave of one of George Washington's cousins, John or Archibald, Brownsville, PA.
(Photo by Martha Hatfield Towns)

I'm honestly not sure if I actually believe in ghosts, but now I realize they were all around me as a kid.

I grew up with an older mother (she was forty when she had me) and a brother eleven years my senior. My dad passed when I was five; so growing up, it was just me and my mom most of the time.

She was crazy about history. Mostly the history of our part of the country (Southwest Pennsylvania), but the rest of U.S. history as well. I don't recall a single vacation we took where she didn't find a Civil War battlefield, or Grover Cleveland's childhood house, or an old cemetery where George Washington's second-cousin twice-removed were buried, for us to visit. I suppose it was her way of adding an educational note to the cacophony of amusement park rides and beach trips. But being significantly older and just a tiny bit wiser now, I think back to those years and I consider how much my mom had lost in her life, and that for her, the past must have been a very comforting place in which to dwell.

I suppose nobody thinks their upbringing is unusual when it's happening, but I was at the very least keenly aware that my childhood was unlike that of many of my friends. The sheer amount of time I spent in old forts and graveyards, or being surrounded with people at least two generations older than me, I'm sure affected me and helped mold me into the oddity I am today.

Because the ghosts were everywhere: ghosts of dead soldiers; ghosts of old Presidents and generals; ghosts of beloved relatives, now long gone. They pressed in on the periphery of my everyday life, like actors waiting in the wings for their cue. I didn't *see* anything as a child- not ever. But I could feel them all around, if I thought about it. I could sense both their sadness and their patient frustration: frustration at lying like an old fossil under the ground, helpless to affect anything any longer. The entirety of my Western PA world- from the decaying coal mining towns that some members of my family came from, to the old growth woods I'd camp in as a teenager- it all overflowed with an undiluted history of conflict and triumph and failure and loss. A great subtle sorrow seemed to me to permeate the whole region, and my friends and their families had no inkling.

But my mom did, and so did I.

Most places I go, if there's a book to be found about local hauntings, it'll be in my carry-on bag on the way home. I'm fascinated by this subject, but I'm also fascinated by people's fascination with it. Ghost stories obviously fill some empty but necessary place in us, to be *this* ubiquitous in our culture, and I hope parts of this book will address that phenomenon.

I hope that, with this book, I can contribute to that uncanny collective with a series of stories that have rarely been told elsewhere. That said, I have several goals concerning the work you now hold in your hands: there are things I want it to be, and there are things I definitely don't want it to be. I want the following accounts to be unbiased and as factual as human memory can be, while being neither didactic nor cynical. I want the narratives to be informative and engaging... and yes, even *spine-tingly*, while avoiding being unnecessarily melodramatic or *trick-endy*.

My ultimate aim is to present to the reader some odd experiences I've personally had, some interesting ones that have been related to me firsthand, and also some of the more bizarre historical legends from my own corner of the country that haven't gotten a lot of nationwide exposure. I hope to avoid stories that rely solely on hearsay, or which can be easily dismissed as apocryphal. My aim is to try- while never pandering to the reader- to tie all these tales together into a single cosmology of oddness- one which never loses hope that there may be more things in heaven and earth than are dreamt of in our philosophies.

If I can depict these thirteen stories seriously, while having a bit of fun in the telling of them, I'll consider my job accomplished. Thank you for reading, and we'll see you on the other side.

Jim Towns
San Pedro, CA
December, 2019

GHOST STORIES

THE LOPING SHADOW

In 2011, I made a film called *House of Bad*. The story followed three sisters (one was a half-sister and that factored into the plot) who steal a briefcase full of heroin from the middle sister's drug dealer boyfriend, and plan to hide out in their remote childhood home for a few weeks until the heat dies down, then head south to Mexico to sell the drugs.

Of course, it all goes wrong. The house contains the trapped souls of the girls' parents, and the family history of hatred and murder (combined with the ghosts) begins pulling the siblings apart.

The film was a small success, and while we didn't have much money for special effects, I felt like we accomplished the effect of the ghostly presences quite convincingly... and there's a reason for that.

I attended the Savannah College of Art and Design from 1992 to 1996, and I enjoyed almost everything about my four years in Savannah- I loved my classes, my professors, college life-- and most of all I enjoyed living in and being immersed in that ancient southern city. Savannah has a long and storied past, being one of the earliest settled cities in the U.S.

Old cities, of course, build up memories over the decades. As the years pile up, so too does the tally of lives lived there- lives of happiness and sadness, splendor and squalor, love and tragedy.

During my time at the SCAD, I had a great professor named Mark Kneece. Mark was an established comic book writer in his how right, and was the Chair of the Sequential Art department. He taught *Writing for Comics* class as well as *Comic Book History*, and I learned a great deal from him. I felt that Mark and I always got on very well, and even though we fell out of touch in the first decade or two after I graduated, we've re-established contact via social media and I'm happy to see he's had continued success in the field.

But this is supposed to be a ghost story.

During the summer before my senior year, I had a morning class with Mark two days a week. Summer in Savannah is the real thing, if you've never experienced it: triple digit temperatures and suffocating humidity, sometimes even at night the air feels so close it's like trying to breathe through a hot washcloth.

We were maybe four or five classes into the quarter, when one morning Mark came into class a bit distracted. In lieu of his usual introduction, he related to us something that he'd seen during the previous night- something that had greatly unsettled him. What follows is taken from Mark's account:

> Mark and his wife were living in an old two-story house on Edisto Island, just north of Savannah. The house was somewhat secluded, and the property overlooked a marsh. They had two small children,

ages four and two, as well as a stepson. During their stay there, his four-year-old son would occasionally talk about seeing the "Shadow Man" in his room at night [editor's note: this was 1995, well before the internet and social media made the idea of Shadow Men a common supernatural trope].

Mark was inclined to write his son's stories off as the natural byproduct of a young boy's imagination- but if he was honest with himself, his son's story gave him an uneasy feeling. From the time they'd moved in, the marsh house had had a creepy vibe, as if someone or something was always watching them. He tried to dismiss the feeling, and was to a degree successful, until the night he himself saw the Shadow Man.

He and his wife slept in an upstairs room, and past the foot of the bed, on the opposite wall, was a row of windows that overlooked the marsh. That night, he was awoken in the small hours by the sound of his wife screaming. Struggling through the fog of sleep, he realized she was shouting that *somebody was touching her*- and then he saw a figure walking along the foot of the bed, silhouetted against the dim nocturnal light coming through the windows.

As his wife kept screaming in terror, Mark was frozen, watching the shape as it crossed along the bedrail. Even as he stared, it turned and started coming up his side of the bed. The figure was tall, and sort of brownish colored- like the color of a paper bag- wearing a coat just past the hips, baggy trousers, and walking in a kind of odd way. Later, he recalled that it walked almost like a cartoon character [he described it to me as being similar to the walk of Robert Crumb's *Mr. Natural*], taking these long, loping strides as it approached him.

The idea that what he was seeing might be a ghost didn't register with Mark at first- he was convinced that there was an intruder in their bedroom. So he leapt out of bed and attacked it with the only weapon he had handy, his pillow. As the shape came at him, he swung at its head- and didn't hit anything. Even as his blow missed, he recalls, the shape retreated to the darkness of a shadowy corner, disappearing fully into the black.

Mark was fully convinced there was a maniac standing there in the dark corner of his bedroom, waiting for him to come too close. Unfortunately, the only light switch on the wall was in that direction, and as he slowly reached for it, he kept expecting the figure to grab him.

A very long moment passed, and after some clawing at the wall and fumbling, he got the lights turned on. There was nobody in the dark corner. No baggy, loping shape. Just an empty corner. The door to the hallway was closed. No one had gone out. There was no other way in or out of the room.

Mark spent the rest of the night sitting out on the dock with a bottle of wine. Without a doubt, something had been in their house- something his four-year-old had seen many times, before it had revealed itself to the adults. Mark figured he might have been dreaming, except his wife had seen the Shadow Man, too. They'd been planning on moving anyway, and now that seemed an even better idea.

They stayed in the house by the marsh for a few more weeks after that, and Mark slept with the light on every night. But nothing else happened after the night they saw the loping shadow. In fact, following this alarming nocturnal visitation, the house seemed to lose much of its creepy atmosphere. Maybe whatever it was hadn't liked being attacked.

A few things strike me about Mark's story. First and foremost is how the details are so burned into his memory- I reached out to him at the outset of writing this book, and his recollection of the minutiae of an event which took place over two decades ago is remarkable. Yes, Mark is a writer and has a natural flair for narrative, but the detailed way he describes his nocturnal visitation is really fascinating.

Second: the loping gait he attributes to the Shadow Man is simultaneously comical and oddly disturbing. Why would someone walk like that? If this *was* some kind of ghost, was this the way that person walked in life? Or was this peculiar stride a post-mortem affectation of an uneasy spirit? It's a curious detail I've never heard elsewhere, and I think it gives this particular haunting its own unique element.

Finally, I recall on that day in class that Mark described the figure as if it carried a permanent shadow with it wherever it moved. Far from the common conceit of the glowing ghost, his spectre seemed to *absorb* light, remaining dim in any situation. This was an element I remembered, and borrowed, years later for the ghosts of *House of Bad*. While we didn't keep the ghosts completely in shadow, my crew and I went to lengths to always have the faces (and especially the eyes) of the actors playing the ghosts to be unlit, perpetually in shadow. My theory was that we read so much in the faces of the people we meet, and in their eyes: identity, mood and, of course, intent. Not being able to see what lay behind the ghosts' eyes made them inscrutable and impossible to read, vaguely inhuman, and therefore dangerous. It's hard to gauge how successful the tactic was in the end, but I thought it was unique, and I myself found it a bit uncanny when we were shooting, so I'll always be grateful to Mark for relating that detail of his very disturbing experience for me to exploit many years later.

THE ATTIC APARTMENT

After graduating from SCAD in 1996, I lived in Philadelphia, Pennsylvania for a year-and-a-half, doing some production design for the stage, waiting tables, and generally just pissing about.

Philadelphia, of course, is a very old town, containing several centuries of human triumphs- and sufferings as well.

An old friend of mine was in his final year of theater school there, and he and I rented a top-floor apartment in an old townhouse on Lombard St., not even a block from its intersection with Broad St., which is one of the main roads of Downtown (or Center City, as it's known). I don't know exactly how old the building was, but in the narrow hallway the moldings were ornate, the balustrade was elaborate and the ceilings were tall in a way that led one to think it had been built before the turn of the Twentieth Century, maybe quite a bit before.

As I said, we took the top floor. The place was about four stories and some change, and navigating couches and beds up the old, curving stairs was some feat. Our apartment had obviously once been an attic of some kind, and had its own door onto the hallway which, when entered, led up a series of eight or ten steps to a small landing. Right of the landing led straight to a living room and small kitchen, left led up a few more stairs to an upper hallway past a bedroom, bathroom and finally to a second, larger bedroom.

My friend and I both worked at a restaurant called City Tavern, which was the same place Jefferson, Adams and Franklin had gone to get hammered after signing the Declaration of Independence in 1776. They had declared themselves traitors to the crown, which came with a death sentence- so a few drinks probably seemed like a good idea. We'd both started as busboys and eventually graduated to be servers. Working there one had to dress in colonial garb and know the stories of the place and generally it was a strange touristy thing and maybe the oddest part of this odd period of my life.

Well maybe not the oddest.

My friend and I both had girlfriends at the time. His was an acting major of Cuban heritage who'd grown up in Florida with a *Santeria*-practicing grandfather sacrificing pigeons in the bathroom sink. She was a nice person, but emotionally pretty mercurial. For my part, upon graduating I had broken up with my college girlfriend of the previous two years, but she wasn't having that and moved to Philly a few months after me, renting an apartment in the very next building. So we were on again. I didn't really have much choice in the matter, it seemed.

I only bring the girlfriends into this story because there was a lot of arguing going on with both couples. Young people in relationships- some of them trying to finish their education, some of them working their first adult jobs. Not enough money. Too much time spent at the bar drinking too much Yuengling lager and way too much Jameson Irish whiskey.

The point is that there was conflict. Heightened emotions and yelling and cursing aplenty. Maybe that's what woke up whatever was there with us. Maybe it would have made its presence known anyway. I can't say for sure.

Again, we had a door to the hallway that led up to our apartment. Directly across from our door was another to the apartment below us. I can't remember the name of its occupant now, but he was a single guy: late middle-aged and was on a pension or disability of some kind. He had a habit of rescuing abandoned dogs off the streets of the city, and so he had a small rotating pack of three or four of various sizes living with him: some medium, one or two tiny ones. All of them were friendly, but they each had that haunted feeling of an animal that's been treated cruelly and even now, with a kind owner, is always wary of people and their capacity for harm.

Whenever my roommate or I left for the day, or came home from school or work, the dogs would bark. We never once entered or exited our apartment without it being accompanied by a ruckus of woofs from the other side of our neighbor's door. I guess we found it annoying, but it was just one of the many quirks of living in the old town: bad plumbing, poor heating, prostitutes hanging out in our doorway. Part of everyday life in Center City.

We'd moved into the apartment in August, and had been there for several months before the feeling became definable (apparently my roommate's *Santeria*-attuned girlfriend noticed something off right away, but didn't bother to share). My own first awareness that something was odd was in January, when I got hit with a terrible flu bug and was stuck alone on the couch for two solid weeks. Anyone who's experienced that degree of sickness knows that one exists in a kind of half-state of consciousness, and there were several times I was aware of someone in the kitchen, a tall figure whom I could glimpse through the doorway out of the corner of my eye, pacing about. I'd assumed it was my roommate, come to get a bite, and would sometimes even speak to him, but he never replied and later on I remembered that he was a germaphobe, and had stayed clear away from the place during my illness. Both the kitchen and figure were blurry and ill-defined from that perspective, and after feeling better I didn't see anything like it for a while.

Then came the night when my roommate and his girlfriend had a big blow up. Another female friend of ours was over that evening and many drinks had been had and his girlfriend walked in on a scene that, while reasonably innocent, probably didn't look good from her perspective. They went up to his bedroom upstairs and there was shouting and swearing and threats and then suddenly, silence. She came downstairs with an odd look on her face. I remember she looked right at me with an almost sorry expression, like she pitied me— then she left. She and my friend patched things up pretty quickly afterward and continued dating for a year or two after, but she never set foot in our place again. He told me that during the argument, at the peak of anger, she'd suddenly gone quiet. She'd looked all around the room, had given him that same pitying look, and turned and walked out without a word.

If you ask me, whatever was living up in that attic apartment with us, which had been more-or-less latent up until then, really got activated that night.

Life went back to a close approximation of normal for a while after that. My girlfriend moved out to the suburbs and away from the ugliness of the city, so I saw her much less. If my roommate spent time with his girlfriend, it was at her dormitory, so the apartment became much more of a bachelor pad. Guys came by to play cards a lot more. Women came over sometimes, but not to play poker. The drinking increased in both frequency and quantity. We worked, we went to the bar, we came home, we partied. The place became much more unkempt and disorganized. The refrigerator contained only beer and cold pizza, and there was nothing in the freezer except a few empty ice trays and a half-empty, freezer burned bottle of Jägermeister.

It was during one of these poker nights we discovered something which changed our entire understanding of this place we lived in. There were four or five of us guys that night playing cards in the living room. One or two of us went out at some point for more beer or liquor or chips or whatever, and upon coming back were treated to the usual chorus of barking from behind our neighbor's door. Evidently this time one of us didn't latch the apartment door properly, because about fifteen minutes after we'd sat back down and recommenced playing, we heard a new cacophony of yelping and barking from below. Getting up to check, I looked down the stairs to the apartment door, and found that it was wide open. I'd had a good deal to drink that night, and so it took me a bit to work it out in my head, but I finally did. I went quietly down our little stairs, out our door and closed it. The dogs stopped barking. I walked down the hallway, paused, and walked back, standing there but not opening the door. The dogs were silent. I took a step towards my neighbor's door and stopped. Not a sound. I made a little scuffle with my shoes. Silence.

Finally I reached out and turned the knob of my door, and heard maybe the slightest whimper from one of the critters opposite. Taking a breath, I opened the door just an inch.

The dogs went crazy.

It all made sense.

They weren't barking at the people coming and going.

They were barking at what was inside our apartment.

I hurried back upstairs to explain my discovery to the other guys, but they were either too drunk or too skeptical or both, and my theory went the way most of the hands I'd been dealt that evening had.

The months went on. The entire place started feeling rotten. It's definitely hard to identify something as truly uncanny when it occurs in the midst of chaos like what we were living in that year. Something died in the walls and our landlord had to break through the living room plaster to get at it, and never really repaired it. My roommate quit his job at City Tavern, so I had to continue dressing up like an idiot on my own. His mother back in Pittsburgh went through a cancer battle that he didn't want to talk about, but he became more and more absent from the apartment, spending his nights at his girlfriend's dorm room. Maybe it was his own personal battle, or maybe it was the toxic state we were living in, but something had finally started getting to him about the place. He mentioned it a few times. His girlfriend had told him something about that night during the argument, and he wanted no part of the attic apartment anymore.

As summer came, I found myself spending any days I had off in the suburbs with my sort-of-on-again girlfriend. I didn't want to be alone in our apartment, especially at night, and especially the downstairs. Five nights a week I walked home drunk from work in the wee hours on the dangerous city streets, past pimps and junkies and gang members- but my own living room terrified me.

As fall came around again my friend and I started spending more time together. He'd graduated and was ready to leave the city for a bit and spend time with his family. I was sick of working at the restaurant, and also I wanted to get out of my old relationship once and for all. I couldn't get any artwork done in our unnerving-feeling apartment, and sleeping there had become almost unbearable. So we decided to pack up and head back home to Pittsburgh for a few months. This decision met with some heavy resistance from our girlfriends, but we were resolved to be out of that place. We gave notice to our landlord, and began packing up our stuff. It felt to me like a huge crushing weight had been taken off me.

There's one night I remember very clearly, only a day or two before we left. It was the night before my last day at the restaurant. I'd been working extra shifts both to save money for the move and also to spend as little time at home alone as possible. I'd worked a double all day, and had an early shift the next morning. I was exhausted. I was dying to get out of there, but that night I had to rest.

It was past midnight. I was lying on my side in bed, facing the wall. Practically all my stuff was in boxes. That evening I'd turned off the lights in the living room, and had then almost run up the steps to escape the darkness. Any lingering pride was gone from me. I was alone in this place and it was dark and I was queasy with fear— but I was also beyond exhausted in body and in soul.

As I lay there I knew someone was staring at me from the doorway. I could feel his gaze in the space between my shoulder blades. It was definitely a he. I lay there for several minutes trying to fall asleep without any success, until finally I summoned the courage to half-roll over. There was a shape silhouetted in the doorway I could see in my peripheral vision. A very tall shape: masculine with broad shoulders, but very slender arms and torso. He was hazy with the distortion that comes from seeing something out of the corner of one's eye, but he seemed to be stripped naked to the waist, with very dark skin. Somehow I knew instinctively that if I rolled fully over and looked at him directly, he would no longer be visible.

The shape stood there motionless, lingering on the edge of my vision- and the eyes I couldn't see bore into me. I spoke before thinking:

"We're leaving," I heard myself say. "We're going away, please leave me alone. I need to sleep. We'll be gone soon."

I rolled back over. I was too tired to be afraid. I don't know if the silhouette disappeared or walked away or if I just finally fell asleep, but I woke up the next day and worked and pocketed my tips and that night I picked up the U-Haul and my friend and I shoved everything we cared about in the back and were ready to go by midnight. We each spent a few hours in the middle of night with our girlfriends for one last intimacy, and by five in the morning were on the turnpike headed away from Philadelphia and that attic apartment.

Coincidentally, that was also the night Princess Diana died in Paris. Someone told us as we carried boxes down our stairs, past our neighbor's barking dogs, and out to the truck.

I got a speeding ticket on the Turnpike on the way home and I didn't care. I was out of that place and that city. I've only been back to Philly twice in the last two decades, and both times I've stayed well clear of Lombard St. It's not that I think it can hurt me in any way, of course. Not from the sidewalk in any case. But I'm a different person now from that guy who lived there in 1997 & 1998, and in a way I'm happy to leave him there with whoever else lives there now- and whoever was still living there when I did.

STRANGERS ON A TROLLEY

It was winter. Winter is one thing when one drives their car to work, and parks in a garage at night. Winter is quite something else when one depends on mass transit every day to get to and from work. Nothing, I've learned, feels quite as cold as standing and waiting on a train platform in January.

It was 2001. I was twenty-six and I had recently moved home to Pittsburgh from New York City with my tail between my legs. I'd moved to the Big Apple to work in comics, but after two frustrating years I'd given up and come home to stay at my mom's house until I figured out my next move. She lived in the South Hills, and I got a job at a temp agency working in Downtown Pittsburgh, just being a long-haired office monkey- filing things, taking messages- dumb stuff. But it was work, and I needed to save up to get my own place.

There was a time when Pittsburgh's trolley system had crisscrossed the entire city. One could get anywhere on a trolley, from Bridgeville to Oakland, from Rankin to Mt. Oliver, Downtown to Sewickley. But at the time of this story, most of those routes had been taken over by buses, and the new Light Rail Transit system (or "T", as it was now called), travelled only one line, from Downtown through the South Hills. My stop was the Castle Shannon station, about a half-hour's ride from the city. From there I'd walk through the woods to my mom's house.

I'd gotten off work late, probably 8:00 or so. So it was fully nighttime when I got on the trolley. I usually liked sitting in the rear of the car, because I'd often read, and I have a thing about people being able to see what book I'm reading. I'm not sure why I care; it's just one of my things.

It being well past rush hour, the trolley car wasn't much occupied that night. On my way to the rear, I walked past an older guy in a suit holding his briefcase on his lap. I remember he had bright red socks showing, and thinking he probably got them for Christmas a few weeks before. There was a heavyset woman in a babushka (which is a type of head scarf commonly worn by Pittsburgh women of Eastern European heritage) sitting a few rows behind the man on the opposite side of the car. Finally, in the second-to-last row sat a young woman-probably in her twenties. She was pale and very pretty, with a bunch of bright red hair tumbling out from under a black winter hat. Naturally, I very much noticed her. But she made no acknowledgement of me. So I sat down opposite and just behind her in the rear-most seat of the trolley, which was already rolling along.

The T is a curious blend of both subway and trolley: it runs underground in Downtown Pittsburgh, emerging out of the tunnel as it reaches the Monongahela River and going across a bridge to Pittsburgh's South Side. One more tunnel through Mt. Washington, and it once more rides above ground like a conventional trolley through Beechview and Dormont, ducking underground again for a mile as it goes through downtown Mt. Lebanon, then back to trolley mode through Castle Shannon and Bethel Park to its terminus at South Hills Village Mall.

    I was going to try to read, but it had been a long day and as we passed under Mt. Washington and emerged to pause at the South Hills Junction station, I found myself re-reading the same paragraph over and over, my mind instantly drifting. So I tucked the book back in my old army rucksack. The Red-haired girl in front of me was reading, but I couldn't see what from my angle (it's possible my nosiness about what others are reading is the reason I'm self-conscious about people spying- and possibly judging- my own selections).

    Rolling uphill now, we passed the Fallowfield stop and cruised along through Beechview's main drag, Broadway Ave. It's a crazy affair where the tracks actually occupy the middle of the road along with car traffic, so vehicles zip in and around the slower-moving (and frequently stopping) trolley car. With the interior lights on, the windows of the trolley naturally become mirrors at night, but if one leans close to the window, their body and head block the light and the view outside becomes visible. I stared for a bit at the cars zipping past by, and the buildings and then townhouses we passed, but anytime I leaned back for a moment, I could see the red-headed woman sitting opposite me in the reflection.

    Once we passed into Dormont, she stood up and began heading towards the front of the car. I wasn't ogling her or anything, but I did see her making her way up, keeping her footing as we bumped along, then slowed to approach Potomac Station. She must have hit the *stop request* button because I saw it pop on. She paid her fare and chatted a few words with the driver. We stopped, the doors opened, and I distinctly remember seeing her out on the platform. I thought that she looked tired, too, as she started walking to the ramp where the platform met the street. Then we were pulling away again, diving between the close-set houses of Dormont before plunging into the tunnel that dips under the swanky affair that is downtown Mt. Lebanon. As we did, I wondered for a minute where the red-haired woman lived. Was it close to the station or did she have a long walk? Did she own a house or rent an apartment? Maybe she didn't live there- maybe she was stopping at her boyfriend's place.

Those thoughts dangled around in my brain as we passed through the darkness of the mile-long tunnel. Usually, as the T travels the distance underground here, the lights inside have a habit of flickering a few times. I don't know why, maybe it's a defect in the track, but they did it on this trip as well, blinking out and then back twice, then staying off for a couple seconds before coming back on. Those few seconds being plunged into almost total darkness are always pretty weird, even for a weird guy like me. I can't help but wonder almost every time what would happen if the train stalled and everyone on board had to walk out of the tunnel.

But the car didn't stall, and we re-emerged out of the total darkness into the more modest darkness of nighttime Mt. Lebanon, passing right through the station without stopping, and continuing on. From there it was only two stops to Castle Shannon where I got off, so I started checking to make sure I had my bag closed up and ready to go. We paused at the tiny stop called Arlington and the businessman with red socks got off, and once we were moving again I mashed the *stop request* button and stood up.

I walked to the front past the Babushka Woman, paid my $1.50, and waited by the door until the car stopped, and the doors opened. Unlike the Potomac stop, where the platforms are on either side of the tracks, Castle Shannon Station's platform is an island in the center of the two rails: so exiting the trolley I was on the opposite side of the train from where I'd been sitting- the redhead's side. I know this because as I began to walk to the stairs and the train pulled out, I saw her sitting in her same seat, reading her magazine. She glanced up at me this time, but I couldn't be at all sure if she was in fact looking at me, or at her own reflection in the glass.

It didn't fully register for a half-second... just long enough so that when I turned for another look, I caught just the briefest glimpse of ruby locks tumbling out from under a coal-black winter hat, and then the tracks turned and my view was obstructed. But I was absolutely sure I'd seen her, sitting on the train- four stops and at least three miles away from where I saw her get off.

I stood there for I'm not sure how long, watching until the trolley's red taillights disappeared around a bend. Maybe it was a minute, maybe only thirty seconds. It felt like my hard drive had frozen, and had to re-boot. Pretty quickly the cold of the January night brought me back, and I started the trek through the parking lot towards the wooded path home.

As I walked along the moonlit trail under tall bare-branched trees, the air was clear and cold. My mind was going over and over what had happened. There were at least three logical explanations, I came to decide, and one very illogical one:

It was easily possible that, tired as I was, I'd fallen asleep for a few moments and had a quick dream that the redhead had gotten off at Potomac station, when she hadn't at all. The problem with this theory was that I was *almost* absolutely sure she hadn't been sitting there in her seat when I walked up to the front to get off at Castle Shannon.

It was also possible (though less likely) that I had somehow conflated two separate trips on the trolley from two different nights. Maybe one night the red-headed girl had gotten off at Potomac, and the next night she'd stayed on past Castle Shannon. This idea had problems, though: it would require that not only she and I had gotten on the same car on two consecutive nights, and sat in the same seats, but *also* Babushka Woman, who I know I passed by when getting off. People work similar schedules and it's not unusual to sometimes see familiar faces on the commute to and from work, but for all three of us to get the same car and the same seats two nights in a row made the third and forth possibilities seem almost likely by comparison.

The final 'logical' explanation was that I'd mistaken what I'd seen. Fatigue or the light on the platform or some combination of the two had performed a trick on my eyes or my brain, and I'd suffered some form of visual flashback- imagining I saw her still sitting there looking up at me, when she'd gotten off several stops back. This possibility seemed slightly more likely given that she had looked at me, while ignoring me when I'd sat down at first. Still, I thought as I came out of the wood and began walking up the residential street to my mom's house, it seemed pretty farfetched. I was tired, yes- but I didn't feel sleep-deprived enough to full-on hallucinate someone sitting someplace when they weren't. I didn't feel physically weakened or uncoordinated, which I remember from college usually accompanies significant sleep deprivation. So that last rational possibility seemed hard to buy, which left me with just the last one - the irrational possibility:

She was never on the train to begin with.

This one is the toughest sell, of course, because it delves into the realm of the uncanny. I could almost believe that I'd imagined an entire person, except for the fact that I *know* I saw the woman interact with the trolley driver when she got off. With absolute certainty, I know that I saw it.

So where did that leave me? I wondered as I crested the top of Crystal Drive and turned left onto Country Club Dr. One more block and I'd turn right onto my mom's street, Audubon Ave., and it would be only a matter of minutes until I was home. Once inside, I worried for some reason that the details of what I'd just experienced would somehow fade- I'm not sure why. But I doubled down on my mental effort to figure out what I'd just seen, trying my best to suss it out before I reached my door.

There are numerous stories about ghostly passengers doomed to ride the same rails or trains, and I was familiar with many of these even in 2001. I'd read about Stockholm's *Silverpin* ghost train, and my mom had played me that old

"Charlie on the MTA" song. The logical jump between being stuck in the repetitive loop of mass-transit commuting and being trapped in some kind of limbo or purgatorial state of existence is an easy one to make. But the Stockholm legend, at least, has been witnessed by multiple people. In present-day 2019, I've done several internet searches to see if anyone else in the Pittsburgh area has ever seen a comely apparition with red locks on the T, and found nothing. So what I saw that night was either my mistaken understanding of something completely ordinary, or perhaps it was just a one-off, a special spectral appearance just for me. To be honest the doubter in me finds that even more difficult to believe than a regular haunting.

I rode the trolley the next night, of course, and the night after and the night after that. I never saw my red-haired woman again. For a week or two, every time I got on a train, I'd check to see if it was the same driver as that night in question, in the hopes that he'd remember a crimson-topped beauty. No luck. The next week after the incident, I thought I saw Babushka Woman on the platform downtown, but I was too chicken to ask her anything.

Time passed and I got a job I could drive to, so no more standing on cold train platforms for me for a while, no more reading on the train (which I miss: I used to get a lot of reading done that way), and, of course, no more chances to spot the ginger enigma. In fact, until the time of this writing I hadn't really thought about her in years. I rode that route hundreds of times, and I remember almost nothing about any of those trips- but every detail of this particular night remains in crystalline sharp focus for me.

Hopefully I'm mistaken. Hopefully I fell asleep or saw something that wasn't there. I'd hate to think of anyone trapped to an eternity of riding the Pittsburgh trolley.

Especially in winter.

MARKS OF A PITCHFORK

El Mirage, California - the Mojave Desert:

My friend Anne and her husband Jesse live up in the high desert. When I first moved to LA in 2005 from the Eastern part of the United States, I found myself in a bit of a dilemma: I write scary stories- for film, or fiction or whatever, it's what I do. Southern California is almost perpetually sunny. It's mostly flat. There are people *everywhere*. There's frankly almost nothing gothic or creepy about it. So how, I asked myself, does a guy who writes creepy stuff draw inspiration from a place like this?

But then I went to the desert, and it all changed.

I'd never been in a desert before. Being from back east, I guess like most folks I assumed that a desert was a desert. I had no idea how diverse and different in both appearance and in actual *vibe* they could be. Some deserts are rocky, while some are sandy. Some are blazingly hot, and some are chillingly cold. Joshua Tree National Park feels like you're either at the beginning of the Earth, or at its very end- the air is so clear and crisp you can see clearly for miles- and anyone miles away can see you. There's a feeling of exposure and vulnerability that I've never experienced in any of the woods of the Northeast. There are things in the desert that can kill you with the utmost ease- and if they can't, the desert can do it all by itself. It's a hostile environment and everything in it has learned to survive that hostility... everything, that is, except you.

Anne and Jesse moved to the desert from Chino, California in 2008. They'd rented a U-haul to transport all their belongings, but as Anne pulled it into the dirt driveway of their new place, the tire sank into the jagged remains of the base of a road sign. There was an audible rush of air from the tire, and they could see it flattened out. They parked as close to the house as possible and unloaded the truck, hoping to deal with the flat the next morning. But morning came, and Anne and Jesse came out to find the tire full of air and in perfect condition. Perfect enough to drive the sixty miles back to Chino to return the truck. This was their first night in the desert: a ghostly welcome.

It was some time later, that someone or something dragged a pitchfork all around their house.

Anne and Jesse were at home watching *The Shining* that night. They had three dogs, and none of them noticed anything strange happening- but after the video was over, they found that a pitchfork had been dragged all around their property, leaving deep furrows in the sand surrounding the house. The tool itself - which was not theirs - was leaning against the side of the house.

While an intrusion like this obviously has a disturbing quality for any homeowner, at first blush this story seems far from anything uncanny, much less supernatural. The answer could be a simple misunderstanding, a disgruntled neighbor, or bored kids.

But there's another element to the story: two weeks prior to this evening's events, two members of Jesse's family had died, and one of them had been planning to purchase a pitchfork at the time.

THE FALLING CHRISTMAS TREE

I'm not sure if this one even counts as a ghost story, but it's pretty interesting.

In 2003 I had a little apartment in Castle Shannon with my girlfriend. In less than a year, she'd break up with me, and I'd move to California and a new chapter of my life would begin. But that was the future; and at the time, this year had been a tough one. I had a very old friend living nearby, whose parents had both been going through protracted battles with cancer- his father had it in his lungs and his mother's tumor was in her brain. It had been months of surgeries and chemotherapy and convalescence and I had been trying my best to be a good friend to my buddy, as he dealt with the long goodbye.

The end had finally come, and his father had succumbed in the early fall, his mother losing her fight in early December.

This double whammy was especially hard, as I'd spent a lot of time at my buddy's place in my teens, and his folks had always been great to me: they'd fed me and driven us all over the place before we could drive, and had generally been another surrogate set of parental units to me. They really were just solidly good people.

So Christmas time that year was a bit of a mixed bag. My friend had lost his mom and dad and, to a lesser but still significant degree, I'd lost people who'd been important in my life.

It was Christmas Eve, and my girlfriend and I had a big tree up in the living room, all decorated with lights and ornaments. We'd gone through some lows in our own relationship that year, as well... but this was a good night. We'd made dinner, and now were drinking some wine, sitting on the floor by the tree. It was a nice moment.

We were chatting about who-knows-what, and eventually our conversation moved to talking about my friend's mom, who again had just passed a few weeks before. I was saying something similar to what I've said above: that she was a heck of a nice woman, and I was grateful to have had her in my life.

And then the tree toppled over and fell on us.

Let me backtrack: we'd gotten the tree at least two weeks before this, and set it up. It hadn't so much as budged in that time. We'd been in the living room every day since then, working near it on our computer, or watching TV. We'd put each other's presents and packages beneath it. It hadn't moved. We'd passed in and out of the room, going from the kitchen to the bath to the porch to the closet, dozens and dozens of times. The tree had never so much as quivered.

I don't really know what to think about it even now, but it was just exceedingly odd, the timing of the thing. I find it hard to believe that the ghost of my friend's mom, sweet as she was, would knock a Douglas fir over on my head- something aggressive like that would be diametrically opposed to her nature in life. And as a self-styled supernatural skeptic, I find it hard to buy that such a thing as a ghost toppling over a six-foot, fully-loaded tree is even remotely possible... but it happened.

I sit here in my living room, three thousand miles away and sixteen years later almost to the day, and I glance another tree that was probably not even a seed in 2003. I'm waiting for it to do something, anything: for the lights to flicker, or a ball to fall.
    Nothing.

EFFIE

How body from spirit does slowly unwind, until we are pure spirit at the end.
—Theodore Roethke

When Tamika was younger, she and her sister lived near Weeds, California with her grandma, who they just called Gram. This was a very rural part of the state, and the house her Gram owned was far away from any neighboring houses, and very old.

Inside the house, there was a portrait of a woman named Effie. Effie had lived and died in the home in the days before Tamika's family came to stay there. Odd things would often happen in the house- lights would switch on and off, doors would open and close- and the family would attribute these oddities to Effie. In Tamika's own words, "She was good for opening and closing doors and turning lights on and off."

By way of example: one day Tamika's aunt had to take her Gram to the hospital, which was almost an hour away. She probably assumed they'd be back before Tamika and her sister came home from school, but that ended up not happening, so Tamika and her sister found themselves locked out of the house when they got home.

> "We did what most kids would do and that was play outside while it was still daylight. As it started to get dark, we sat on the stoop in the back with the dog. We could hear the phone ringing inside, but had no way to get in to answer it.
> When the sun had set, I noticed there were lights on in the house and the door was ajar. We were never afraid of Effie because we never got a sense of anything bad. I just assumed with it being dark, Effie had turned on the lights and let us in the house. We went about our business until my aunt got back, and told her that Effie had let us in. When we moved from that house into town she went with us."

While many modern people put little faith in anything that smacks of the supernatural, others have no issue whatsoever acknowledging the existence of a paranormal world which borders (and sometimes interacts) with ours. And just like anything else, there are many more folks whose belief lays somewhere in the middle of these two poles of credulity. Surveys have shown that between 42 and 62 percent of adults in the U.S. believe they have in some way made contact with someone who has died (*Omega- Journal of Death and Dying, 2006*).

The belief in things that can't be explained is and has been a central component of human existence from the beginning- the concept of a world existing beyond the reach of human understanding lies at the base of almost every major religion and spiritual belief system; and traditionally, those who had access to the world beyond - oracles, soothsayers, mediums and their like - were seen by their respective cultures as being of a special and valuable class of persons.

The one absolutely inescapable reality of human existence is that, at some point, it ends. The longer we're alive, the greater the number of loved ones and friends we outlive. We accumulate loss throughout life until, eventually, the weight of that loss can seem almost too much to bear. *Any* hope that there exists a world beyond ours- call it Elysium, or Heaven, or Summerland- helps to mollify that feeling of grief. Whether one regards them as faith, spirituality, or merely a coping mechanism, these beliefs allow us the promise that death is possibly *not* the end, but rather just another step in the evolution of our spirit.

The house Tamika and her family now live in near Pottsville, PA is over a century old. They've been told it was previously owned by a man who lived there with his daughters.

An aunt from California came for a visit once, and slept in an upstairs bedroom. She woke in the middle of the night to find a man in high-waisted pants in her room. With him was a girl in a white nightgown. They said and did nothing, but only stared at her. The aunt refused to sleep upstairs for the duration of her stay. Tamika's sister has seen a woman sitting in a chair watching her, and her sister in-law has seen unexplainable figures moving about in the hallway. Tamika's mother told her that one night while she was lying in bed, it had felt like someone had crawled into the bed behind her- it scared the life out of her.

Nocturnal bedfellows aside, the family co-exists with these other residents in reasonably good humor. The most annoying part seems to be that their silverware often goes missing. For a long time Tamika's mother was convinced that family members were somehow throwing the utensils away, and would repeatedly go and buy new cutlery, only to find the original silverware returned every time. So she's stopped buying new forks and knives.

She just waits for them to be returned.

AMERICAN CRYPTIC

JIM TOWNS

BOOGEYMEN

JIM TOWNS

THE SIX-TOED MAN

I was in Boy Scouts for several years, but I was never anything close to resembling a poster boy for Scouting- I had long hair, listened to heavy metal, and fooled around quite a bit with girls. I remember part of the Scout Oath had to do with being *physically strong, mentally awake, and morally straight*. At least I got the mental part right.

But I really enjoyed the outdoors part of Scouting. My troop would camp out one weekend almost every month (even in winter), and that's what I was there for: hiking, making fires, and spending time in the quiet and simple remoteness of nature. We'd travel all around Western PA and Maryland to camp in State Forests and local campgrounds- and once a year we'd spend a week at *Heritage Reservation*, a Scout camp about two hours south of Pittsburgh.

> From Heritage Reservation's official website:
> *First opened in 1980, Heritage Reservation has been the premier destination for Scouts and Scouters of*

Laurel Highlands Council and beyond. The Reservation is home to Eagle Base and Camps Independence, Liberty, and Freedom, as well as a year-round conference center available for all to use. Main attractions for campers include 270 acre Lake Courage with over six miles of shoreline, excellent shooting facilities, and nearly 2,000 acres of beautiful mountain woodlands.

Heritage really was beautiful. The lake was big enough to canoe, row and even sail on. There were merit badge classes on everything from basket weaving to pioneering to model rocket launching. Several troops would camp there at a time, so it was an opportunity to meet kids from other parts of the region. But arguably, everyone's favorite activity happened one night each year. It was called Outpost. Outpost was when select (usually older) members of the troop would canoe across the lake to stay on the uninhabited side for a night. It took at least a half-hour to an hour to make the trip. You were allowed to bring a sleeping bag, food to cook, and knives, saws and axes for cutting wood- but there were no tents allowed. You had to build your own shelter for the night and sleep in it. It was a test to prove you could make it a night in the wild- even if that wild was only a mile away from camp.

It wasn't that rough. Once landing on shore, there was a rush to get a lean-to built or at least string a tarp up overhead in case of rain, but once that was accomplished, Outpost was a lot of fun- again it was mostly the older teenage kids and some adults, and for me at least, it was a night away from the more martial side of Scouting: a night to build a roaring fire and huddle around with friends and make Mountain Pies, to tell bad jokes and sing tasteless songs- and, of course, to share spooky stories.

I first remember hearing about the Six-toed Man from the older boys when I was still too young to go out on Outpost, and while I don't think I fully grasped what it was those guys were talking about, I was aware that this person they were speaking about was some kind of boogeyman- someone out in the woods whom one needed to watch for if they were spending the night away from the safety of the camp. On my first Outpost, however, the real terror the Six-toed Man embodied became evident, as after the fire burned low and we were all settled into our crude makeshift shelters, shivering a bit even in the summer night, we all started hearing things: a rustle in the grass nearby; the sudden pop of a log on the fire; or a twig snapping somewhere beyond the edge of the treeline; or a canoe suddenly shifting down by the shore, its bottom keel making a harsh *scrape* on the stones. Panic is contagious, and each unidentifiable sound elicited a chorus of teenage exclamations that fed back into a widening loop of fear. I feel bad for the adults amongst us who had to deal with a dozen thoroughly freaked out adolescents that night, all of them sure that at any moment the Six-toed Man was going to emerge out of the darkness and snatch them away.

Huddled inside my sleeping bag and listening for any sound of approaching (possibly misshapen) footsteps, it never occurred to me to wonder how anyone in our troop had learned about the existence of this Six-toed Man character. I didn't think to question if he was some kind of regional legend, or possibly a creature conjured up solely out of the culture of the camp. In the intervening years, I'd begun to suspect that he might have been just a creation of one of the Troop's leaders or members' imaginations, or that maybe the Six-toed Man had some kind of place in real history, and was something one of them had heard about once. It turns out that last hunch was probably correct:

What follows is based on the account of a Mrs. Ruth Canfield, a member of the Historical Society of Venango County, which is north of Pittsburgh (in the opposite direction from Heritage Reservation, for anyone wishing to keep track). This narrative is taken from what seems to be a local hand-printed periodical called the *Keystone Folklore Quarterly*. For the purposes of its inclusion here, I've taken the liberty of rewriting some parts of Ms. Canfield's original text, as it was written in the 1960s and contains outdated racial and social references: rest assured the below text maintains all of the original narrative details:

During the American Civil War, there were a string of farms in Western Pennsylvania that served as stops on the Underground Railroad, helping liberated enslaved persons on their trip towards freedom in Canada. Amongst these way stations was a farm in Rockland Township that was owned and operated by a well-to-do gentleman named Elihu Chadwick Jr., who was "very dedicated to the cause of Freedom and to the freeing of the [...] slaves in the South."

> *Two other way stations... one in Butler County across the Allegheny* [River] *from Emlenton to the west of the one in Rockland Township was the stop before coming to Rockland. The escapees coming from other stations would travel by night and with the aid of local people, cross the river and make the Rockland stop by daybreak, remain over the day in hiding, or for several days until they were rested and fed...*

Elihu Chadwick Jr. and his wife Isabel Jolly Chadwick were in their mature years during this time, and amongst their seven children was one boy (James) who'd enlisted in the Union Army in 1861, and one daughter who was developmentally disabled.

The legend goes that among the African American fugitives who came to the Chadwick place was a young man who had six toes on each foot- a condition now referred to as *polydactyly* or *polydactylism*. For one reason or another, the elder Chadwick decided to keep this young man as a houseboy.

> *After a time it seems he (the boy) made improper advances to the girl, and one of the brothers promptly shot him and the family disposed of his body in an old water well in the stock barn that supplied the animals with water, and filled it up with stones.*

Ms. Canfield's narrative states that the freed youth made advances on the daughter. If the story is indeed factual, the truth of what their interaction was might prove forever elusive - the salient detail is that something happened between the polydactyl boy and the girl that caused the boy to be murdered, and his body discarded.

> *It would seem the community knew about the incident but was either unconcerned or didn't want to make any trouble for the "great man" in their midst. But the tale was told and retold by the oldsters when I was but a small child...*

This is how legends begin: both the mythic stories of heroes, and also folk takes about boogeymen. A larger-than-life figure falls, tragically, and then rises again. The nature of the story - if it's to be a myth or a fable or a ghost story- depends mainly on what happens next:

> *...and in the telling and retelling no doubt much was added to the story and later the ghost of the six-toed [man] wandered around the vicinity of the Chadwick Farm and wailed at the old well filled with stones.*

In these types of colloquial narratives, tragic characters have a tendency to become ghosts, destined to re-enact their unfair deaths over and over throughout years and decades and centuries, seemingly out of a compulsion to remind the living of their tragedy. But boogeyman stories like this one are used for something else, as well: and have been since our species told oral histories in front of sputtering fires, listening for the sounds of predators lurking just beyond the flickering light. Boogeyman stories are used as teaching tools, a kind of social propaganda employed to scare and intimidate people (especially youngsters) into doing what is desired of them- arguably for their own good:

> *...the legend of the six-toed man served as a strong weapon in the hands of mothers and father- as a deterrent to keep their small ones from wandering from the home domicile. I well remember our families warning us if we strayed far in the woods or away from home we would no doubt meet up with the "colored ghost" which would be the end- so needless to say, we heeded the warning.*

The next morning of Outpost, we were all present- no one had become the Six-toed Man's latest victim. If this particular legend is indeed based on historical fact, then to me it has two very sad overtones: the first of course being the senseless waste of a young man's life, someone who'd successfully escaped enslavement in the South, only to die at the hands of the very same ignorance and racism still extant in the North.

The second crime committed against this poor soul was the appropriation of his tragic story into a campfire tale used to scare youngsters- one that trivializes his death but ignores and forgets the unjust manner in which it occurred, and which uses as its main identifier a congenital anomaly this young man likely dealt with his entire short life. But for that physical oddity, Old Man Chadwick would likely have ushered him on to Canada and his story might have been different - if not so notorious and legendary. If nothing else in life, we can all hope that we don't become little more than a cautionary tale.

Legends about polydactyl peoples have been around almost as long as civilization: a Giant of Gath with four extra digits is mentioned in the Book of Samuel. A people referred to as the Melungeons - thought to be stranded Sixteenth Century Portuguese explorers who migrated inland to the Tennessee Valley- were said to have extra fingers and toes. And in 1895 the remains of what was supposedly a twelve-foot giant were unearthed in County Antrim, Ireland- complete with extra toes. For one reason or another, polydactylism has, for much of history, forced many of those encumbered with it into a separate class: in some eras they have been regarded to be noble or sacred, a conduit to higher powers; but often people with this condition have been considered simply *the other*. This 'otherness' phenomenon seems endemic to our species. It crosses cultures and continents and centuries.

So what is it in our human brain that has so often inclined us to treat anyone possessed of such a small physical difference with such awe, or with such fear? Is it jealousy, that these people were seen as having something extra- something regular twenty-digit people would never be able to understand? There's obviously some deep-seeded psychological trigger there, which has caused polydactylites across human history to be relegated into one of these two categories: more than human, or less. There were no accompanying details to the Six-toed Man legend we were told - no stories of what he did or why he was something to be frightened by. The simple idea of a person possessing this unusual trait was enough to terrify us as we slept in our makeshift shelters that night: one salient detail which by itself should not have been frightening, but which made this character we'd been warned about a thing apart- and something to be feared. A fresh tragedy piled atop another, older tragedy.

A final paragraph in the Ruth Canfield story swerves abruptly into an entirely different local story with little connection to the legend of the Six-toed Man, but it serves to set up an upcoming chapter, so I include it here:

> *It was thought by many people in olden times that the Chadwick place had been either a popular hunting or battle ground of Indians. What tribes I do not know, perhaps the Senecas or the Cornplanters- for to the present day arrowheads are often found by farmers on the old Chadwick place and adjoining properties. Several miles away there are evidences of "mounds". A neighbor told me he had opened one or two of the mounds but had found nothing of any consequence.*

THE PARK DEVILS

> Like one, that on a lonesome road
> Doth walk in fear and dread,
> And having once turned round walks on,
> And turns no more his head;
> Because he knows, a frightful fiend
> Doth close behind him tread.
>
> *-The Rime of the Ancient Mariner*
> Samuel Taylor Coleridge

My friend Amy Park Woodall and I go back a ways. She and her husband Manfred, along with Tamara Moore, owned the Pittsburgh gallery I used to show my paintings in from 2000-2005, and we all enjoyed some great times and big successes together. In addition to being a business owner, she's a successful writer, editor and publisher.

And apparently at least four generations of men in her family have seen the Devil.

Amy grew up hearing stories about her ancestors' encounters every year on New Year's Eve. It began with her grandfather William Park, who'd grown up in Scotland before coming to America in 1913 at the age of 24, so this first account would have taken place sometime around the late 1800s or early 1900s when William was still a young man. She relates it thus:

> "He was walking home alone one dark night along a lonely road, and he heard footsteps coming up behind him. He looked, but no one else was on the road. He walked on but still heard those steps following behind him; he'd look again, but still see no one there. As he started to walk faster, they moved faster. He started to run, and the footsteps raced after him. He finally reached his home and ran inside, slamming the front door, and as it slammed shut behind him, he heard something hit against it on the other side. His parents were home and heard it as well, but when his mother opened the door, nothing was there."

Now in fairness, this narrative of sinister footsteps following a lone traveler on the road is a familiar story: in addition to the above Coleridge stanza, it's reminiscent of the fable of Stingy Jack (the mythic origin of our modern Jack O' Lantern), the Nineteenth century account of unfortunate Frenchwoman Louise Le Sénéchal, Washington Irving's *The Legend of Sleepy Hollow*, and even the legend of bluesman Robert Johnson. However, I'm not sure if this isn't one of those cases where the frequency and familiarity of a tale repeated again and again over centuries of storytelling don't actually *add* something to its credibility, rather than impugn it.

If true, then whatever it was pursuing Amy's grandfather down that lonely road that night must have followed him to the

New World, because decades later in Pittsburgh, his son John Park (Amy's father) tells a story of when he was home in bed alone, sick with a fever. In the middle of the night he rolled over, and found someone lying next to him.

"Who the hell are you?" John yelled.

"You know who I am," the being laughed. Her father knew; he said it was the devil.

More decades passed, and Amy's brother John had his own frightening encounter:

> "My story begins on a dark, moonless night. I was of college age and was driving home from dropping the young lady who would become my wife off from a date. It was very late, and for some reason my mind was thinking about the event mentioned above. At the spot where the beating had taken place, I looked off to the side of the road, and saw something that totally changed my ideas about evil.
>
> There are not many things darker than a grove of crab apple trees on a moonless night. But back in the total darkness I saw a figure standing that was darker still. As I saw this figure, I got very cold. It was however different than any cold I had ever felt before. Instead of the cold flowing from my extremities and radiating inward, this cold began in my bones, and flowed outward into my body. And at that moment, whatever there was in me that was "good" recognized that what I was looking at defied any form of logic. What I was looking was a physical darkness that held a cold of its very own. What I was looking at was purely evil."

Several years later, Amy's nephew Michael revealed that he'd had an eerie dream:

"...there was nothing really terrifying at the time, but only much later as I slowly realized what had happened that it became so deeply unsettling. I remember that, in the dream, I was sitting with a man over coffee or tea or some other "proper conversation" beverage. He was dressed well, like an Olde Gentleman of some kind, although without a particular region or time-period attached to that feeling, which was eerie. I don't remember what we discussed, but I remember waking without any feelings of ill-will or such similar things. It was slowly over time that it was like my heart realized I had been duped, and from that realization a slow, creeping darkness rolled out from inside that memory as the truth came into being. Certainly, for me, the strangest part is that I don't dream anymore, and that it happened so cleanly with this encounter. I can never seem to properly describe the sensation of closing my eyes exhausted, and immediately opening them up, like all that I had done was blinked, to feeling well rested with an alarm clock going off. I don't have a sensation that time passed, and I don't have what people and movies describe as that fleeting memory of a dream already forgotten. I just blink, and my energy is restored and somehow it's 7 or 8 hours later..."

Two things become clear, if one is to take these accounts seriously:

First, whatever this devil or specter is, it definitely seems to have some kind of issue (or fascination) with the Park family.

And second: either it's able to change its form at will, or else it's evolving.

Amy and Manfred live outside the city in an impressive Mid-century Modern house on a hill. The top floor, with its floor-to-ceiling windows, looks out over a swath of woods running down into the valley below. They have neighbors, but the house has always felt wonderfully remote to me. The bedrooms are on the lower level of the house and face outward to the woods as well, so the hallway connecting them runs along the inside next to the hill and below ground, almost like a tunnel. And while Amy is not one of the Park men, that hasn't kept her from being visited by terrible visages in the night, even in the safety of her own bedroom:

> "... one night I had a dream that felt unlike normal dreams. I dreamt that I was in bed and got out to look down the hall. The light was on in the hall—there was something very odd about the light and the atmosphere, like it was vibrating or the color was wrong or it had some extra mass to it. There was a man coming down the hall. I remember being filled with fear and it felt like it was taking so very long for him to approach, but I knew it was going to be very bad when he reached me."

> "I had a similar-feeling dream again a couple of years later. Everything was the same—this time I stayed in bed, but the light in the hall was the same and I could sense this figure getting closer this time. Then the man came into the room. He sat on the foot of the bed and leaned in over me, and his face began to vibrate and morph.
> And as he was leaning closer and closer to me, I started yelling "Who the f--k are you?! Who the f--k ARE you?!" at him. I was so terrified. Manfred woke me up because I really was trying to yell in my sleep, but wasn't getting it out."

Of course it's very possible that these two visions Amy had were nothing more than dreams, and it's also likely they were influenced by the stories she'd heard about William, John, her brother and her cousin's experiences. But she can't recall ever having nightmares of the intensity that she did on these two nights.

Also, later on her husband Manfred had a dream that he woke in the middle of the night, and turned in bed to find a man crouching over Amy on all fours.

THE GREEN MAN

Pittsburgh's legend of The Green Man is one of those myths that has grown and mutated over the years in the repeated retellings, absorbing elements from other stories and amalgamating them into its own mythology so that it contains narrative tangents that seem wholly unconnected to the source story, and are difficult to trace backwards. Everyone, it seems, has their own version of the Green Man's origin and appearance, his purpose and powers. Much of this conflicting information is easily found on the Internet, yet can be tricky to dissemble.

The story begins in 1919, when 9-year-old Raymond Robinson was growing up in the Beaver Falls area, an hour north of Pittsburgh. Wanting to see if there were eggs in a bird's nest, he climbed up a pole on the Morado Bridge and came in direct contact with un-insulated trolley wires. Raymond was severely injured:

BOY BURNED TERRIBLY THROUGH HIGH TENSION- coming in contact with live wires carrying about 25,000 volts of electricity on the Morado bridge, Raymond, about 13, son of Mrs. Mayme Robinson, a widow woman of Morado, was probably fatally burned last night about 8:30 o'clock. He was rushed to the Providence hospital by Dr. George L. McCormick and is still living today, but without hope of recovery. He is said to have climbed on a box on the bridge of the Harmony route at Morado after a bird's nest, when he came in contact with a coil of wire. He was terribly burned about his hands, face and eyes, and his eyes were literally burned out.
Immediately his predicament was discovered, and he was given prompt attention.
About one year ago Howard Latell, aged 10, son of Mr. and Mrs. Harvey Latell, was burned in much the same way and died later in the Beaver Valley General Hospital in New Brighton.
   -The Daily, Beaver Valley, PA, June 19, 1919

As the article states, another boy had been electrocuted and died just months before in a similar incident, and both doctors and newspapers expected young Raymond to likewise succumb to his injuries, but he would prove them wrong:

DOCTORS MARVEL THAT BOY LIVES- LAD NEARLY ELECTROCUTED ON WAY TO RECOVERY- Raymond Robinson, aged 8, his eyes burned out and his body mangled, will yet live to tell the story of how it feels to receive 11,000 volts of electricity through one's body, according to word from the Providence Hospital, Beaver Falls, where he has been for about two months since his experience.
The boy was reaching for a bird's nest on top of a pole at Morado bridge, along the Harmony route

street car line, when his hand came in contact with a lightning arrester carrying 11,000 deadly volts. There was a blinding flash and he was hurtled to the ground.

For weeks he hovered between life and death after being removed to the hospital, retaining his senses all that time. Now the doctors claim he will live. The boy's hearing has not been affected and he talks readily enough. However, only two holes remain where his eyes were. One of his hands is gone and both arms are in bad shape. The upper part of his body shows marks of severe burns. Yet, in spite of all his affliction the boy is in good humor, though he has nothing to say of the occurrence.

He is the son of Miss Anna Robinson, a widow woman of Beaver Falls. He is the second victim of an accident of the kind.

   -*The Daily Times,* Beaver County, PA, August 16, 1919

Despite the inability of the local papers to agree upon Raymond's age, his mother's name, the way he got up to the wires or the voltage of the shock he received, the common facts add up to a small but tragic miracle - Raymond survived. The accident left him blinded, disfigured and handicapped (most accounts list him as having lost his right arm and much of the use of his left). And while no mention is made in the newspaper accounts, there must have been an incredible amount of pain the young man had to deal with during his recovery, and likely the rest of his life, as well. He was given a pair of darkened glasses with a prosthetic nose attached to wear, and went home with his mother. He seems to have resided in the same house for much of his life afterwards, looked after by family. Years passed. He learned to read Braille. He crafted leather goods like belts and wallets to sell. He mowed the lawn with a push mower. And then at some point, he started going for walks, and this is where the legend of the Green Man began. It's also where things start to get confusing.

Raymond walked mostly at night, likely so as to avoid encountering people. He continued his late night perambulations for decades, supposedly all the way up to the 1980s when he was a septuagenarian. His favored path was Route 351 between Koppel and New Galilee- a narrow and winding two-lane road. He'd keep a hand on the guardrail that ran along the road as a way to keep safely out of the way of cars, but there are accounts saying he was hit more than once by passing vehicles.

There's mention that during these walks, he'd often attempt to hide from sight when he heard people approaching, but something happened over the years. Maybe the isolation got to him, and he wanted to meet people and interact with them (remember, his hearing and speech- as well as, presumably, his mental facilities - were unaffected by the accident). Whatever the case, Raymond started talking to folks in cars- mostly youngsters- who would stop to speak to him, and word about him began to spread in the area. As it did, teenagers began making a habit of driving along the route at night in hopes of spotting the burned man, and Ray would often chat with them and sometimes even pose for photos in return for beer and cigarettes the kids would offer him. There are stories about the local police having to be present some nights to keep the flow of curious cruisers hoping for a glimpse moving, and at least one account of them ticketing the cars of kids who parked in the hopes of chatting with Ray.

As the years passed, people (perhaps not familiar with Ray's tragic story) began referring to him as Charlie No-Face, and this moniker became an established part of the Green Man story. How Raymond Robinson became known as the Green Man, however, is a bit trickier:

Green Man Tunnel, South Park, PA
Photo by the author

"The legend goes that he roams that hollow late at night and chases the parkers and the loafers... I never saw him. Right now, it's a big topic in the high school. ... The legend is still strong."
  -Marie Werner, Elizabeth, PA

"The guys used to take their girlfriends there, you know... and scared them half to death. Of course, I never parked in that tunnel."
  -Jo Pelesky, South Park, PA

   The location now commonly known as Green Man Tunnel is on Piney Fork Road, in South Park, PA: 54 miles away from where Raymond Robinson was injured and spent most of his life. There are actually two tunnels close together- cutting through a hill underneath the tracks of the old Baltimore & Ohio Railroad system that used to transport coal from nearby mines. The larger of the two tunnels is where the road passes through, but a few hundred feet away is another opening in the hill- in later years it's been used by the township for storing salt for winter road clearing, and the inside passage is completely filled by a mountain of dirty white crystals. The opening itself is partially obstructed by huge cement blocks, stacked like gargantuan Lego bricks. Barely visible above the arch '1924' is carved into the stone. The outside is absolutely covered in graffiti: images of green-shaped figures pop up here and there, and *Green Man's Tunnel* is written in several places.

These are not old vandalisms. They're fresh and new. The legend of the Green Man is alive and well in locals' minds, even if it bears little connection to the man upon whom it's based.

Local folk legend says if you drive through the tunnel at night (presumably the passable Piney Fork one), stop midway through and flash your lights and honk your horn, the Green Man will appear. This, by the way, is extremely dangerous to do, as the tunnel is only one lane wide, and the road just on the far side of the tunnel makes a sharp turn; so there's no way to see what's coming towards you from the opposite direction, or for any oncoming traffic to see a car stopped ahead in the middle of the tunnel.

It's uncertain how the locus of Green Man stories came to land here, an hour's drive from Route 315 (there are also versions of the story that put the site of Green Man's hauntings in the North Hills, Brookline, and even Washington PA), but it's here in this rural area that it's come to rest, and it's here its legend has grown.

Like its setting, origin stories about the Green Man vary wildly: most agree that he suffered an accident that disfigured him, but many versions depict him as a railway or power company worker. The cause of that disfigurement is also up for much interpretation: He was struck by lightning. He was burned with acid. Some versions come close to the truth, portraying him as someone who was shocked by a downed power line. Likewise, the stories don't agree on what the immediate result of the accident was. In certain versions the man was killed outright and the Green Man seen walking the road is his ghost. In other iterations he retreated to an abandoned house to live out his days. Through some kind of dubious scientific process, the lighting (or electricity or acid) made his skin glow green, giving him the name Green Man. As near as most can pinpoint it, this evolution of the story began in the 1950s, when Raymond would have been in his forties.

These iterations are obviously more colorful than the historical truth, and it's easy to understand why they would catch on- omitting the child element, they lack some of the tragic nature of the historical account, and are therefore easier to be thrilled by. They also lack some of the complexity of the true narrative, and perhaps that makes them easier to be digested and repeated as well. This, again, is an essential part of how tragic true-life figures are transformed over time into boogeymen - like the Six-Toed Man before him, the real-life personage of Raymond Robinson must first be stripped of much of his humanity, in order to fit into a very narrow archetype. Often, this transfiguration requires the characters to be somehow complicit or at least partially to blame for their own fate, and that might explain the Green Man's transformation into an adult victim rather than a boy: after all, an adult (especially one working near electricity or acid or other dangerous elements) should have known better or been more careful. The function of this particular form of victim-blaming is likely to divorce the listener of the boogeyman story from any strong feelings of pity, which would dampen the fear factor of the tale. It seems that this dehumanizing is an unfortunate but often necessary side effect of the cultural process of mythologization. Something is lost, so that something new can be created.

Raymond Robinson died in 1985, at age seventy-four: he lived for sixty-five years after his accident. He was buried in Grandview Cemetery near his home, but the legends surrounding him didn't end there.

In December 2019 I visited the Green Man Tunnel along with my friend and co-filmmaker Mike McKown, and took photos and video. We drove through the Piney Fork tunnel and paused, honking our horn and flashing our headlights to see if anything appeared. It did not. Maybe it was because it was daytime, or maybe it was because the legend of the Green Man has absolutely no basis in either fact or experience - a mangled mess of oral history and urban legend.

We spent some time standing in front of the Green Man Tunnel proper, and I *will* say that it, along with the entire area nearby, has a palpable unnerving quality about it. The location is remote and out of the way of much traffic, but there's a strong feeling that everyone who does pass through the area is fully aware of what it is, and what it represents- even if that means something different to each person. But that's the enduring strength of a myth - unlike a historical account, myths can adapt themselves to suit each person's taste, yet remain intact over years and decades and centuries, if only a few key factors remain consistent.

So maybe mythologizing is a way we as people deal with stories like Raymond Robinson's: stories that are almost too sad to endure. By converting them into the archetype of fable, we make them palatable. It's difficult to live in a world knowing that at any time random tragedy can strike, illness can arise out of nowhere, and natural or man-made disasters can happen without little or no warning. Storytelling creates a structure from this raw material, incorporating the key elements of truth into a construct that feels not only balanced, but also fateful. Things happen for a reason, everything has its proper place in the cycle of life, and the dead can sometimes still speak for themselves.

INDIAN PETER

AUTHOR'S NOTE: this chapter contains numerous instances of the word "Indian" in reference to both First Nations groups and individuals. This outdated term is used here only in the interests of accurately conveying the wording used by the story's original narrators.

Indian Peter would get you, she was told. He would get you and take you up to his Indian Fort on the hilltop, and you'd never be seen again.

Brownsville, Pennsylvania is a tiny little town hugging a hill on the banks of the wide, slow-moving Monongahela River. Believe it or not, there was a time when folks didn't believe Pittsburgh would ever establish itself as a city, being so close to the industrial metropolis that was Brownsville.

Brownsville's primary purpose involved a step in the steel-making process many people don't know much about. Most of us are at least vaguely aware that steel is made from iron ore, which is then heated to remove impurities. A small amount of carbon is added, depending on the type of steel being manufactured. The temperatures needed to melt iron are extreme, and that's where coke comes in.

Not *Coke* like the drink: coke is a product of taking coal and burning it in a space without oxygen. This remakes the coal into almost pure carbon - like an industrial-strength charcoal briquette. Coke is what's used to make the fires hot enough to make steel, and the hills around Brownsville were once littered with rows and rows of tiny coke ovens (if one imagines a brick igloo, they'd be close). The coke was transported downhill to the waterfront, and there loaded onto barges to be transported downriver to the mills in Pittsburgh. So Brownsville was a vital part of America's steel industry from the Nineteenth Century all the way up to the 1970s.

But then the steel industry died. And with it went much of Brownsville's purpose for existing as a town. A large mall opened up on the hill by the highway, and folks moved out of town looking for new kinds of work, because as The Boss himself so succinctly said: *These jobs are going, boy - and they ain't coming back.* Present-day Brownsville still exists, but only as a shadow of what it once was.

My mom, of course, grew up in the town's heyday. Down the river, Pittsburgh was churning out steel for the War effort, and Brownsville was a vital part of that. Her father (and her mother after him) served as the town's Tax Collector, and their family was well known in the town.

It was my mom's older sister, my Aunt Eleanor, who told her the scary stories about Indian Peter:

> "Eleanor used to kid about somebody was up on the hill... Indian Peter. He scared the little kids... and truly there was a Peter St. in Uniontown named for him...

he was a real person... But according to Eleanor... he would just appear anytime."

Despite the fact that many people from the Brownsville area I've spoken to are aware of this particular boogeyman legend, the only information I've been able to find about this character pertains to an actual historical figure, known alternately as William Peter, Peter Redstone, or Indian Peter:

> *It is related in Crumrine's valuable and well written history of Washington County, that the land upon which West Brownsville stands was originally owned by Indian Peter. This Indian Peter, at a very early day, lived on lands in the vicinity of Uniontown, and gave name to Peter's street, the oldest street of that town. He had a neighbor whose name was Philip Shute, with whom he was not on friendly terms. Prior to 1769 Indian Peter wrote to the authorities of the proprietary government, that "he could not get along with the damned Dutchman, and wished to give up his land for another tract." His request was promptly complied with, and he was given a tract of three hundred and thirty-nine acres, situate on the west side of the Monongahela river, which was surveyed and called "Indian Hill" and upon this tract stands the town of West Brownsville...*
>
> -Thomas B. Searight, *The Old Pike, a History of the National Road, with Incidents, Accidents, and Anecdotes Thereon* (1894)

Not only was Indian Peter a real personage, it seems he played a role in both the founding of Brownsville as a town as well as the negotiations between European settlers and the Native tribes who had called the area home for millennia:

> *On Sabbath, the 27th, of March (1768), a considerable number [of European settlers] attended... and most of them told us they were resolved to move off and would petition your Honor for a preference in obtaining their improvements when a purchase was made. While we were conversing we were informed that a number of Indians were to come to Indian Peter's. We, judging it might be subservient to our main design that the Indians should be present, while we were advising the people to obey the law, sent for them. They came, and, after sermon, delivered a speech, with a string of wampum, to be transmitted to your Honor. Their speech was 'Ye are come, sent by your great men, to tell these people to go away from the land, which you say is ours; and we are sent by our great men, and are glad we have met here this day. We tell you, the white people must stop, and we stop them till the treaty, and when George Croghan and our great men talk together, we will tell them what to do.' The Indians were from Mingo town, about eighty miles from Redstone (a little below Steubenville).*
>
> - James Veech, *The Monongahela of Old: or, Historical Sketches of South-western Pennsylvania to the Year 1800* (1910)

The picture that emerges from these records is one of some chaos: a provincial government attempting to placate the local Mingo tribe in an effort to keep the peace, and simultaneously attempting to control their own people's custom of seizing Native American property through force or intimidation. All the while they (the provincial government) were working towards a treaty that would appropriate the entire region for England.

The Provincial Assembly of Pennsylvania then passed the drastic act of February 3, 1768, providing for the serving of a thirty-day notice to vacate, and in cue of failure so to do, "being thereof legally convicted by their own confessions or the verdict of a jury, shall suffer death without the benefit of clergy." Soon after the passage of the law Governor Penn appointed... a committee to visit this area and warn all of the settlers off the lands by May 1, 1768... They came by the Braddock Road from Fort Cumberland to Gist's Plantation, and then by the Burd Road to Redstone. A meeting was held here, attended by some Indians from Mingo, who encouraged the settlers in their demands that they remain on the lands until a treaty was effected... The Indians at the conference were Indian Peter, Captains Haven, Horneu, Mygog-Wigo, Nogawach, Strikebelt, Pouch, Gilley, and Slewbells.
    -Lewis Clark Walkinshaw, *Annals of Southwestern Pennsylvania, Vol. 1* (1939)

Again Indian Peter is at the center of momentous events in the area. The picture painted is of a man who somehow managed to walk between both worlds: Native and European, and was respected by both as an arbiter and an advocate. There seems to be little information explaining how Peter grew to become this local character of stature, except for this extract from a letter sent to England in 1762:

IN my way from the warm springs in Virginia, I lodged at Fort Frederick, I came to the Fort about 6 hours after Indian Peter, and a white woman, his wife, left it. This is their history:
The woman was taken prisoner about two years ago, just after a bloody action between the Pennsylvanians and Indians, in which several of the Indian chiefs fell ; at such times they rarely forgive their prisoners ; the

> *poor woman, was sentenced to be tortured by fire for three days, and was actually tyed for that purpose when Peter came up, and offered a very large reward for her ; they refused to listen to any terms, so great was their resentment : Peter then insisted they should release the woman, and accept of him as a sacrifice to the manes of his deceased countrymen. It is said, the Indians dare not refuse to release a prisoner on such terms; she was untyed , they did not care to burn their countryman, whom they all liked; they then bargained with him for 100 buckskins, 500 pieces of wampum; and six horses, a great price. They were on their way down to Pennsylvania, to settle by her mother's.*

This account portrays a man of almost heroic qualities- one willing to gamble his own life in order to save an innocent, but also cagey enough to judge a situation and the people in it. Perhaps it was these qualities that led Peter to be a key player in the dangerous dealings of his era.

Thomas Searight caps Indian Peter's story thus:

> *Indian Peter, it seems, died in possession of the Indian Hill* (West Brownsville) *tract, and it passed to his widow Mary, a white woman, and his oldest son William.*

All this above information is interesting, but it leaves a dangling question: how was this historical personage transformed over the centuries into a character intended to frighten children? Here is a figure of some historical prestige, a man who'd obviously earned the respect of many - a husband, father and founder. Nothing in the factual record of Peter Redstone AKA Indian Peter indicates tragedy, as in the stories of the Six-Toed Man or Raymond Robinson. Indian Peter wasn't a victim of an untimely death or a disfiguring accident.

But Indian Peter does share something with the two other boogeymen - his otherness.

Even during his life, Peter's popular moniker served to announce his different-ness from the white people with whom he coexisted in relative harmony (with the possible exception of his German neighbor). It seems likely that, in walking between two worlds, Indian Peter found himself belonging wholly to neither.

A myth is a story told over and over, a little different every time. This particular type of myth- the boogeyman- needs to hold up to a very basic emotional logic: one that balances on the intersecting axes of life, death, injustice and tragedy. Something happened at some point, and it wasn't right or fair, and thus we have this result. Peter Redstone's life eschews any indication of these factors being present, so his rendering into the boogeyman mold feels forced and ill-fitting. Maybe that's why no one seems to know how this transformation came to be.

Without a clear understanding of the stages by which the mythifcation of Indian Peter happened in the oral history of Brownsville, most of this is at best inference, and at worst educated conjecture. But considering just the documentations I've found about the real Peter's life, one thing is clear: his story is complicated, and- as discussed in the chapter on The Green Man, complication is something we don't enjoy in our boogeyman myths. Perhaps it was simply easier and more satisfying for tellers of spook stories to simplify the man Peter into a vague specter - a creature with the singular intent of grabbing unsuspecting children and whisking them back up to his fort (allegedly the old Redstone Fort mentioned in the accounts). There seems to be just enough story there, just enough flavor of the exotic, to generate the fear reaction desired in the story's intended audience. And maybe that's all that was necessary for the legend to outlive the man.

AMERICAN CRYPTIC

JIM TOWNS

UNCANNY PLACES

THE DEER CORPSE GOD

As I said, I used to camp quite a bit, both with the Boy Scouts, and, as I got into my teens, on my own or with friends.

I don't remember which park I was camping in, but it was down in southwest PA, almost near the Mason-Dixon Line. It might have been near Amity, Pennsylvania, but my recollection isn't one hundred percent on the location.

The rest of the memory, though, is very clear.

I was sixteen or seventeen. I was in the woods, alone. It was summer and daytime, and I remember I was on some kind of mission. I could have been trying to find wood for my fire, or I might have been hunting for arrowheads or something. I was walking along the side of a large hill, and the terrain was convoluted, with mossy boulders sticking up everywhere and fallen and decayed tree trunks crisscrossing my path. At one point I put my boot on a rock and either I slipped or it gave way beneath me, because the next thing I remember was being flat on my back a few yards down the slope, having slid to a stop.

I was in a little declivity between the rocks that a trickling flow of water had cut, so I was below the level of the ground, and my hind end and the bottom half of my legs were soaked with cold water. It all happened really fast, and it was one of those things you need to be careful of when out in the woods. I wasn't far from camp, but I hadn't told anyone where I was going, and I doubt anybody had paid attention to which way I'd set out. I didn't have food or water with me, as I hadn't expected to be out long or trek any great distance. But if I'd broken a leg, or knocked myself out, it could have been quite some time before anyone missed me, and much longer before they found me. Even on a summer night it's possible to get hypothermia up in the mountains.

Luckily, a quick check convinced me I was fine: just a little shaken, bruised, and wet. I got hold of something and stood up. My exploring was over for the day - time to go back to camp and change into dry clothes. But as I stood up, I came face to face with a deer.

His face was only inches from mine. He was dead, and had been for a few days, at least. His eyes had clouded over all blind and green, and a half-inch of purple tongue lolled out of the corner of his mouth. His brown fur had faded to an ashen grey and what had been a dark black snout at the tip of his narrow nose had now bleached out and turned spotted with red.

It was beyond my knowledge to determine how long the creature had been dead, or what had ended its life. It might have been a hunter, but I didn't see any blood. The poor critter might have been sick or old and just finally given out right here by this little brook. Oddly, the corpse didn't have the familiar reek of decomposition for something in its state of decay.

The surprise of what I'd come face to face with stopped me for a few seconds, while my brain caught up processing it. For all the (obvious) signs of corruption spreading through the deer's body, it still seemed likely that the animal might just get up and dart away from me. I was still wet, and I needed to get back to camp, yet a part of me felt bad leaving it here, alone. But I knew that was silly. This was the way of things. This is where he belonged.

I was about to turn away, when I noticed the insects.

They were so tiny that it was easy to miss them at first. They were about the size of ants, but they weren't ants- they lacked that familiar segmented body type. There was a long row of them, probably hundreds of the little guys in a single-file line. The line led up from under a mossy lip in the rock, up to right in front of the deer corpse's nose, then away again in the other direction, and back under the stony shelf. Many (not all, but many) of the insects approaching the deer's nose carried things: little pieces of green, hazy pink pieces of flower or bits of pollen. I thought I saw a tiny pinpoint piece of a mushroom even. The insects would walk up to the face of the dead animal, and place the things in front of it, before turning away to follow the procession back under the rock again.

I was staring at this for some moments, trying to figure out exactly what I was looking at. My first impression was that it looked an awful lot like a wake, and these insects were paying their respects to the fallen creature, offering little gifts as tokens of their esteem. That was what it looked like, but of course that couldn't be right. Insects don't mourn the dead, and they certainly don't mourn the dead of a species so vastly different.

A second theory occurred to me- could they be trying to help the deer, maybe not realizing it was too late, and offering it little bits of sustenance to help it heal? But that made no more sense than the wake theory. The way the insects approached, single file, with their offerings- then laid them before the giant head of the deer- it almost seemed like a sacred ceremony. Like worshippers laying sacrifices before a deity. Had these bugs somehow decided that the rotting cadaver of the deer was their new god? It's an absurd concept. But for all the world, that's what it looked like.

I needed to get back to camp.

As a culture, we have a compelling need to see every mystery solved. Much of our entertainment is based on the solution of problems or mysteries. In the real world, we devote untold amounts of human and financial resources to rooting out problems or questions: scientific, medical, criminal, and eliminating them. We lean heavily into the relief that comes with resolving a question to our satisfaction: learning the whys and hows, the underlying causes and the ultimate rational answers. It's intrinsic in our natures, it seems, to want this satisfaction, and unanswered questions are the stray dangling thread that continues to bother us.

I didn't mention my experience to anyone back at camp. I wasn't sure how I'd describe it, and anyway it started with my own clumsiness, which was embarrassing. And also, it probably bothered me that I didn't understand what I'd seen. I didn't like not having the answer, and so I stayed quiet about the deer and its little friends. Maybe there's a perfectly logical scientific explanation for the curious ritual I'd witnessed, but in all the years since, I've never come across it. And also, as I've gotten older, I find that I'm more comfortable *not* understanding it.

JIM TOWNS

THE OLD ASYLUM

B etween 2003 and 2005 I co-directed my first feature, a retro-silent era film called *Prometheus Triumphant: a Fugue in the Key of Flesh*. A mouthful of a title and a handful of a project, it took several years to shoot. To create the film's forsaken and decayed settings, we used a dozen old locations around Pittsburgh, PA: abandoned steel mills, condemned houses, even parts of the University of Pittsburgh's famed Cathedral of Learning.

And, of course, we shot in Dixmont Hospital for the Insane.

Built in 1862, The Western Pennsylvania Hospital for the Insane (the place went through several names in its century of operation) was inspired by the vision of a woman named Dorthea Dix. In the 19th Century, Dix was an advocate for the mentally ill, and championed the creation of what would become the American mental institute system (before this the mentally ill in the United States were mostly confined to almshouses where treatment and therapy were all-but absent). It was built in the Kirkbride fashion, similar to Danvers and many other facilities constructed around this period- a main building, several stories high, which ran lengthwise for hundreds and hundreds of yards- offering seemingly endless hallways. Soon the institution took her name and was (for the time) a state-of-the-art facility treating Pittsburgh's mentally ill. Thousands of patients and hundreds of employees lived and worked on its sprawling, 400-acre campus, complete with many ancillary buildings, kitchens, laundries- even its own cemetery. My understanding is that for many decades, even up to the mid-20th century, the hospital provided a reasonably humane and caring refuge for most of its patients, before financial troubles caused the State of Pennsylvania to take over the private institution in 1946. With State control came electro-shock therapy, lobotomies and worse. Dixmont continued on for a few more years as better mental health care caused its patient population to dwindle, until it finally closed its doors in 1988. After that, the great old building sat empty by the banks of the Ohio River, and time and the elements slowly took their toll.

It was a news article in the Pittsburgh Post-Gazette that my co-director Mike saw in 2003- a feature about the old hospital about to be demolished to make way for construction of a Walmart- that first got us thinking about filming at Dixmont. We'd been making another film, also of the silent German Expressionist type, but that one had somewhat fallen apart. So on Easter Day, I put together a costume with a long coat, top hat, and a creepy white mask, and we snuck onto the property to film some test footage. That footage came out really impressive; the shots we were able to get of the main building's crumbling façade were incredible, something we'd have never been able to build or otherwise create. Time had ravaged the place, but had also changed the geometry of its architecture with what seemed like perfect aesthetic vision.

After our initial guerilla scout, we secured the proper permissions and paid the proper fees in order to be allowed onto the property to film legitimately (our cast and crew had to sign waivers due to the asbestos and other harmful materials which had been used in the buildings over the years), and we spent several days shooting there. I remember the majority of that time being enjoyable, albeit in the very stressed gotta-get-all-the-shots-done rushed kind of way that is filmmaking. After our first camera tests, we'd looked at the footage, half expecting to see phantom images that the camera caught which we couldn't see, or even for the video to be garbled for no reason - but it was fine. Crisp, in focus captures of the vast decrepitude all around us.

We mostly shot in an adjacent building known as the Dietary building, which had a vast pillared hall that had been used for meals. The room (and Dixmont as a whole) had been the victim of some graffiti spraying and general vandalism, but that was the only part of it we had to cover or fix. Otherwise, once we had our cast dressed and in makeup, we were able to film without doing a thing to alter the set. Things went very well on the first day, during which we actually shot much of the film's finale... although we did have one scare:

The plot of *Prometheus Triumphant* combined several classic horror concepts into one, but rested heavily on a Bride of Frankenstein-type story about Janick- a disfigured doctor who, during a plague, finds a way to resurrect Esmeralda, the woman he loved before he was scarred. When she's brought back to life, it's as if she's newborn again, so the actress playing Esmeralda spent much of this particular day completely naked, but for a coat of white body paint. We were filming in August now, and it was very warm outside, but inside the old stone building it was very cool - maybe cooler than it should have been. At one point I turned to give her some direction, and realized she wasn't able to understand me. She was shaking under her blanket, and we had to carry her outside. Apparently, standing on the stone floor, the cold from the building had crept up through the soles of her bare feet, and brought her body temperature down to a dangerous level. It had happened so fast it seemed... unlikely, but there she was sitting in a car in August with the heater blasting. We were much more attentive after that.

And then I had my moment.

I played the male character for much of the film (we had another actor play him when his face was intact). Luckily I got to wear clothes in my role (well, except for one scene, but that's another story). The mask I wore was, as mentioned, a plain white one, but it had thin black material glued onto the inside to cover the eyeholes, so the eyes of the character were just black voids. The material was see-thru, but it did limit vision quite a bit, and of course the holes themselves were small and offered very narrow windows to see what was around, so negotiating any physical movement while wearing it was a challenge.

It was the last day of filming at Dixmont (we still had much of the rest of the film to shoot in other locations). We needed a shot of the character peering out from his ruined refuge, and I had the idea to go up inside the main building to the top floor (the third) and look out one of the open windows at the end of the edifice, while my co-director filmed from outside and below, a few hundred feet away.

I hadn't really thought about it- we'd gotten pretty comfortable shooting at the asylum, the group of us. I'd rarely been alone in the building up until now. Of course, this only occurred to me as I was climbing the stairs. The first flight of steps was relatively clear. The second flight had quite a lot of debris on it. By the time I was making my way up the third one, there were almost no steps visible- just a steep ramp of dust (and probably asbestos). I found myself on all fours struggling to clamber up.

The windows at the end of each hall of the gigantic building had been large, from floor to ceiling, and from wall to wall. There was a small ledge maybe a foot high on the floor. Of course the glass of the window was long gone, so I found myself standing thirty feet above the ground below, with only a tiny little lip as a guardrail. And my back was to the vast, quarter-mile long hallway behind me. Then of course I had to put my mask on, so I couldn't see anything, and stand there while we shot the shot.

Those were long moments, standing there as the camera rolled. Up until now I hadn't *felt* anything at Dixmont, maybe just a dull sadness, but nothing acute. Now, however, I felt a cold anger behind me- nothing localized into a specific form or person, just a deep well of what felt like frustration, resentment (For the doctors? For the living?) and fury. A hundred years' worth of human beings had been forced to live out part their lives here. Many had died here, as the cemetery attested. I stood there thinking how it would take only a gentle push and I'd have nothing to grab onto. I'd be one more casualty of this place.

The camera cut. I was able to take off my mask. I turned around - just a long, lonely empty hallway cluttered with detritus. But the feeling was still there. I made my way back downstairs and outside.

Dixmont was torn down two years later, with the intent to finally construct the shopping plaza there, but the hill it was on proved unstable and unsafe for building, so now the place is just empty. I haven't been back since that day we filmed the window scene. I'm told nature has taken the area back over, and it's quite pretty there, now. I'd like to visit it again someday. It was an important moment in my life and career- one that set me on a path that's led me to Hollywood and many more film projects since. If and when I *do* go back, I feel very sure that- demolition or not- I'll still be able SEE the great big building standing there, the way it was when we filmed: a relic that had outlived its purpose- now as much a thing apart from the world as the souls that inhabited it for so many years.

THE GIANTS UNDER THE MOUNDS

...it was a tradition of the Indians that the first tribe occupying this whole country, was a black- bearded race, very large in size, and subsequently a red bearded race or tribe came and killed or drove off all the black beards, as they called them."
- *The Firelands Pioneer*, 1858

We were driving through Uniontown in my mom's Buick station wagon when she first mentioned the giants who'd lived in the area before the White Man came, and were buried under great earthen mounds all around. I was maybe nine or ten, and the idea filled my imagination with fantastic images of ancient lost cultures - and also the strangely hopeful feeling that there were always more secrets waiting to be uncovered.

First off, the facts:
During the time known as the Early Woodland Period

(roughly 1000 to 200 BCE) the area between New York and Missouri was home to a population of between eight and seventeen million indigenous people collectively known as the *Adena*. The Adena were hunters, agrarians, traders and artists- but the most prevalent reminder of their existence are the remains of hundreds of earthen mounds, or *tumuli*, they built as tombs for the dead. Ranging from twenty feet across to over three hundred feet in diameter, many of these mounds still stand today in Ohio, Kentucky, West Virginia and Pennsylvania.

Adena Mound, Ross County, OH.
Photographer unknown (possibly William C. Mills)

Spearhead Mound, Anderson Twp, OH (destroyed in 1940)

Customarily, stone vaults would be constructed to hold the remains of the chosen dead, and the body would be interred along with a collection of grave goods: pottery, combs, and sometimes jewelry. Then basketfuls of earth and clay would be piled around and atop these crypts, creating a first layer. Later on more vaults would be built on top of this original layer, and similarly filled in, eventually creating the mound shape.

These mounds were objects of some surprise to European explorers and settlers in Pennsylvania and Ohio, who could not believe that the indigenous people would be capable of such architectural accomplishments. And in truth, mound building technology had passed mostly out of the area (along with the Adena) more than two millennia before the first white man set foot in the Ohio Valley, so the Native Americans colonial settlers encountered in the Eighteenth and Nineteenth centuries had little knowledge to share about the people who'd built the mounds thousands of years before. A Native elder was quoted in an 1883 issue of *Scientific American*, saying: "We know nothing about them. They were here before the Red Man."

The accepted scientific estimate of the average Adena ranges between 5'6" and 5'11"- which is still relatively tall for a people who existed before the Roman Empire. In keeping with this estimate, modern archeology does not accept the theory that some Adena females grew to be over six feet tall, and some of the males to between seven and eight feet in height.

And yet, the last 150 years have left us dozens and dozens of accounts attesting that many of them did. Between 1840 and 1960, from New York, Pennsylvania, Ohio, West Virginia, Kentucky, Illinois, Louisiana and Florida, there are over a hundred newspaper reports chronicling the discoveries of humans of larger-than-average height and build, many of which share similar physical abnormalities as well. Following is a series (by no means complete) of contemporary articles relating to the discoveries of enormous bodies buried in these mounds:

> *"This mound, which was originally about 100 feet long and more than 12 feet high, has been somewhat worn down by time. It is on the J.R. Secrist farm in South Huntington township...The most interesting feature in the recent excavation was the mummified torso of the human body...Portions of the bones dug up and the bones in the legs, Prof. Peterson declares, are those of a person between eight and nine feet in height."*
> -*The Sun* (Hummelstown, PA), December 8, 1893
>
> *Bridge Carpenters on the N. & W. R. R. found a gigantic skeleton while excavating, three miles east of Portsmouth, a few days ago. The skeleton measured, 7 feet, 4 inches...*
> -*News Herald* (Portsmouth, OH), January 3, 1895
>
> *One of the three recently discovered mounds in this town has been opened. In it was found the skeleton of a man of gigantic size. The bones measured from head to*

foot over 9 feet and were in a fair state of preservation. The skull was as large as a half bushel measure. Some finely tempered rods of copper and other relics were lying near the bones.
   -*New York Times*, December 18, 1897

Workmen unearthed half a dozen skeletons, most of which were eight feet tall and over. One in particular was that of a man of great stature and all were far above the height of tall persons. Two of the skeletons were those of women. In the graves were found pieces of pottery, such as were unknown by the Indians, which leads to the conclusion that the bones are those of people of a prehistoric race.
   -*Bluffton Chronicle*, July 22, 1903

"Dudley A. Martin, octogenarian and collector of Indian relics, states that he was present at the opening of some curious burial mounds on the Cornplanter Indian reservation in Warren County nearly fifty years ago. These barrows were walled up inside and had outlets to the air, so much so that on opening one mound it was found to be full of rattlesnakes...In one mound was found the skeleton of a chief seven feet tall, wearing much barbaric adornment and jewelry."
   -*Altoona Tribune*, January 27, 1937

In 1932, archaeologist George Fisher began exploring a mound called *Pollock's Hill* in Washington County, PA, after learning it was being looted by amateurs. On September 14th, 1932 the *Pittsburgh Post-Gazette* reported on one of his discoveries:

> "One of the skeletons of these mighty men is seven feet, five inches in length, and even the remains of the women and children show them to have been of tremendous stature. Heavy, primitive faces must have topped their mammoth bodies, Fisher says, for all of the skulls are heavy boned, with massive jaws and strong teeth that could have ripped meat into shreds..."

The remains of more than forty people from Pollock's Hill were sent to the Smithsonian Institution in Washington for analysis:

> *One skeleton making the trip with Cadzow to the capital is a giant 7 feet 5 inches in height.*
> *-Pittsburgh Press*, October 12, 1932

While it's easy to dismiss reports like these as being from a time when sensationalism was often the standard practice for journalism in the United States, these articles, along with the field notes and reports written by contemporary archeologists, contain a consistency of description that's difficult to summarily dismiss:

> *Near the original surface (of the mound)... lying at full length upon its back, was one of the largest skeletons discovered by the Bureau agents, the length as proved by actual measurement being between 7 and 8 feet.*
> *-12th Annual Report of the Bureau of Ethnology*, 1880

> *The Remains of burial 40 is one of the largest known to Adena; the skull-foot field measurement is 84 inches (7 feet)."*

-William S. Webb and Charles Snow, *The Dover Mound*, 1959

When measured in the tomb his length was approximately 7.04 feet. All the long bones were heavy and possessed marked eminences for the attachment of muscles.
  -Don W. Dragoo (Carnegie Museum), *Mounds of the Dead*, 1963

Modern medicine defines gigantism as a condition created by an overactive pituitary gland (hyperpituitarism), causing excessive growth of the skeletal structure during the growing years. The condition is usually accompanied by muscular weakness, and often carries the promise of a shorter lifespan to those affected. To be classified as a giant, individuals must be more than 7 feet in height.

But many of the archaeological accounts from the digs describe the discovery of broad shouldered, heavy boned individuals very dissimilar to the modern humans for whom gigantism is an affliction:

Six feet above these remains was found the partial skeleton of a man almost a giant in size... the breadth across the shoulders, with the bones correctly placed, was nineteen inches.
  -Warren K. Moorehead, *Primitive Man in Ohio*, 1982

Not only were these Adena People tall but also the massiveness of the bones indicates powerfully built individuals. The head was generally big with a large cranial capacity.
  -Don W. Dragoo (Carnegie Museum), *Mounds for the Dead*, 1963

They also include descriptions of elongated or hyper vaulted brachycrany (an abnormal elongation of the top of the skull), along with jaw and tooth structure unlike that of modern humans:

> *A recent exploration of a mound near this place resulted in some interesting discoveries... The form was large, the jaws Massive, and the teeth perfect.*
> -*American Antiquarian*, Vol. 2 No 1- 1879

> *7 skeletons, placed in a sitting position, were uncovered from a burial mound near Clearwater, Minnesota. The highly unusual skulls had double rows of teeth in both the upper and lower jaws. It was also noted that the foreheads were low and sloping, compared to "normal" human skulls.*
> -*St. Paul Pioneer Press*, June 29 1888

> *Only a few mounds, there; one of which was near the C. Wilgus mansion and contained a skeleton of a very large person, all double teeth, and sound, in a jaw bone that would go over the jaw with the flesh on, of a large man.*
> -*Ironton* [Ohio] *Register*, 1892

> *Deformed as* [the remains] *are, these crania display a pronounced brachycrany... it may be noticed that four skulls... displaying submedium deformation, also give an average cranial index of over 90%. Thus the inference is that these people would have shown pronounced brachycrany even without deformation.*
> -H.T.E. Hertzberg, *Skeletal Material from the Write Site, Montgomery County, Kentucky*, 1940

Hertzberg's account suggests that in addition to having

naturally elongated skulls, at least some of the Adena practiced cranial deformation rituals, similar to those performed by the ancient Maya and Inca tribes of Central and South America. If true, this fact would add credibility to a popular theory that the Adena migrated *northward* up into the Ohio and Mississippi Valleys from the South. This migration theory has the potential to explain not only the similarity of head elongating habits, but to also establish an anthro-architectural connection between burial mound culture and Mayan pyramid building. Because it seems it was a general custom of the Adena to cremate their dead, so these mounds are actually a bit of an anomaly.

One theory proposed seeks to explain the disparities existing between what archaeology tells us about the typical Adena (5'7" average, typical skeletal structure, cremated their dead) with these larger-than-life reports of giants with aberrant physical traits: that these mounds were not only built, as we see in Central American tribes, as resting places for some kind of noble class or royalty, but that the skeletons represent an entirely different species of Adena. An elite class, whose greater stature could have caused them to be worshipped by their normal-sized kin.

This sounds like fantasy, of course- the idea of a race of giants reads like something out of Erich Von Däniken's *Chariots of the Gods*, and this work makes no such speculation about alien-inspired civilizations. But the similarities in size and atypical dentition reported in these finds argue that many of these people could have shared similar genetic traits: so if they weren't an entire different taxonomic classification, could they have been part of an ongoing genetic mutation (possibly even one perpetuated through the kind of inbreeding typical of royal lines), which resulted in the perpetuation and even an increase of these abnormal traits?

The fact that this 'giant' phenomenon goes largely unknown and unacknowledged, while so much information on the subject is readily accessible, is in itself very interesting. Naturally, there is a dedicated cottage industry of researchers writing on this obscure subject, led most prominently by authors Jason Jarrell and Sarah Farmer (*Ages of Giants: a Cultural History of the Tall Ones in North America*). But even a vague awareness of this topic seems mostly cloistered around the western PA/Ohio area.

This subject has also had a long history of opponents, most notably one Ales Hrdlicka, who was the founder and first Curator of Physical Anthropology for the U. S. National Museum (now the Smithsonian) from 1903 to 1942:

> *"And the 'giant' and 'eight-foot' skeleton is to this day the almost stereotyped feature in many an amateur report of a find of skeletal remains..."*
> -Ales Hrdlicka

The Bohemia-born Hrdlicka cuts a controversial figure: he was a staunch proponent of the theory that Central Europe (relatively close to his hometown) and not Asia, was the place of human origin- in contrast to many of his contemporaries. Many of his theories are cited as influences in the American government's eugenics programs of the early 20th century, and he's now widely denounced for his callously disrespectful treatment of Aboriginal tribal remains.

During his tenure, Hrdlicka used all his clout to quell any evidence or theories that ran contrary to his own. Dr. Warren King Moorehead, a contemporary of Hrdlicka who was interested in studying the giant remains the Smithsonian had collected, but found upon visiting the museum that the skeletons were suddenly 'unable to be accounted for'- once stated:

> *"Instead of diffusing knowledge, it* [the Smithsonian] *has steadfastly refused to allow its vaults to be opened to scholars from other museums, state*

and local institutions, and any independent research—especially if the intent is to search out anomalies."

But even though at times its gatekeepers can seem inflexible, the wonderful thing about science is that, like many of the subjects it studies, science itself grows and evolves, taking in new information and adjusting theories to accommodate these fresh findings. It would be interesting to see what might be learned if any of the remains mentioned above were to be subjected to modern CT scanning, measuring and DNA sequencing. Would it prove the legitimacy of these accounts? Or would it merely prove the untrustworthiness of 19th century antiquarians and newspapermen? Until that day comes, no one can say for certain. Meanwhile, these skeletons sit in storage somewhere in the basements of the Smithsonian, Carnegie and other great museums of the East, while the rest of their kin still silently rest in the earth under the mounds, keeping their secrets.

AFTERWARD:

I've learned many things in the writing of this book. I've had a chance to re-examine several fantastic stories I'd heard as a child or teenager, hold them up to the light of day and apply some more mature reasoning to them... only then seeing how well they stood the test of time.

Because this is why we tell stories in the first place: real ones, created ones, histories, myths, legends, fables, and sometimes even lies. There is always a hope that the story will catch on, and go beyond the boundaries of our own life- lasting longer than us, traveling further than us. In this way we have a chance to preserve not only a snapshot of ourselves, but of our own unique viewpoint. *I was here. I saw the thing. This is the way it was.*

Scientists call this phenomenon the Observer Effect- the idea that anything a person witnesses, they to some degree influence as well. In research circles this concept is a bit of a cautionary tale: an admonition to attempt every means in order to get a true, unbiased conclusion. But storytelling is a little different. It's nearly impossible, even in non-fiction, to completely remove the writer from the writing. The two are intrinsically linked. Prose is personal, even when its purpose is to be factual and impartial. *We* are the context through which we witness the world around ourselves, and its events. Like rushing water, one can struggle against it, or one can go with it. Some of the tales I had been told as a youngster I found to have solid purchase, and they are included here. Many did not, and had to be left to the mercy of the current. Perhaps downriver somewhere, they'll find a rock to cling to, or a branch to make their way to dry land. Perhaps they won't.

We influence the stories we tell, and we're each of us a unique and complex mix of traits both good and poor: curiosity, dedication, patience, frustration, jealousy, and a hundred thousand more. So if all stories are told from a point of view, and each of our points of view are different, then no two stories- even if they're about the exact same subject - will be exactly the same.

Myths and fables (and yes even ghost stories) enjoy a particular longevity because they're malleable, and can be reshaped to fit this individual context of their storyteller, free of the burden of facts and dates and, god forbid, truth. This makes them both powerful, and like any powerful thing, potentially dangerous. Folk tales can oftentimes dress themselves up as truth, or history, but they have a very different purpose. Rather than to purely inform, their intent is to elicit a specific reaction in the listener or reader: like awe, or pride, or terror. And the strongest of these stories affect us not just on an intellectual level, but a physical one as well. A stirring speech can move its audience to cheers...or anger. A powerful folk story can bring tears, and any good ghost story gives its audience a chill up the spine.

Because there's intellectual truth, and then there's emotional truth- and they are frequently not the same thing.

Maybe the most interesting part of this work for me was discovering the truth behind some of these stories, and comparing it to the legend to see how much overlap the two have- how easily they share the same space. The things I learned are mostly included in the preceding stories, mainly that in order for history to become myth, it usually has to be whittled away at, until the story is just a basic framework onto which each successive storyteller can hang their own chosen dressing. In this whittling process we lose much of what was true or real, but what's gained is a new narrative versatility, which allows the story to go on and on, changing a little bit with each telling- like a game of telephone - a living, evolving thing that can potentially live forever. Not a hundred-percent real, but not entirely fabricated, either. A shadowy thing lurking in the mind or on the shelves, waiting to steal our attention away for a few moments, in order to fulfill some basic need we humans have to be thrilled, or moved, or even just distracted.

We each tell our own stories, and in doing so, we each perform our own unique magic upon our audience, whether it's across the flickering flames of a campfire, in ten-point typeset on a faded white page, or a small glowing screen in the dark. The stories we share unite us, and remind us we're all part of a larger narrative that goes on, and on.

Thank you for reading! If you like the book, please leave a review on Amazon and Goodreads. Reviews help authors and publishers spread the word!

To keep up with more Anubis Press news, join the Anubis Press Dynasty on Facebook.

ABOUT THE AUTHOR:

Jim Towns is a writer, filmmaker and artist. His films include the silent expressionist feature *Prometheus Triumphant: a Fugue in the Key of Flesh*, the necromantic dark comedy *STIFF*, the haunted heist film *House of Bad* and the post-apocalyptic drama *State of Desolation*.

His published short fiction includes "Warlock's Eye" (FunDead Publications), "Fools at the Feet of a Hanged Man" (Dodging the Rain literary magazine), "Castrato" (Things in the Wall), "The Grave" (Hellbound Books) and "Bad Coffee and the Bomb" (Switchblade Magazine). Two of his non-fiction stories included here ("The Attic Apartment" and "The Old Asylum") have previously been included in Anubis Press' anthologies *Paranormal Encounters* and *Handbook for the Dead*.

His paintings and mixed media artwork have been exhibited in galleries in Pittsburgh, New York and Los Angeles.

He currently lives in San Pedro, CA with his wife and two mysterious cats.

ACKNOWLEDGEMENTS:

Special thanks to these people, without whom this book would likely never come into being:

Jacob Floyd
Jenny Floyd
Stuart Conover / The Horror Tree
Mark Kneece
Amy Park Woodall
Anne-Marie Lefever
Tamika Ahlfeld
Chip Towns
Ron O'Shea
Bryan Campbell
Ted Tarka
Noah Nagg
Thomas Monovich
Marc Henshaw

Extra-special thanks to my wife Betty Lou Sedor, who was there all along in this endeavor with advice, support and encouragement. This book would not have been possible without you.

BIBLIOGRAPHY:

Charles Almanzo Babcock, *Venango County, Pennsylvania: Her Pioneers and People*, Vol. 2, J. H. Beers & Co., 1919.

Bob Batz, Jr., *Legend of the 'Green Man' Glows Anew*, Pittsburgh Post-Gazette, October 30, 2018.

Edmund Hayes Bell, *Echoes of Early Brownsville*, Historical Society of Western Pennsylvania, 1924.

Ruth Canfield, *The Tale of the Six-toed Negro*, Keystone Folklore Quarterly, Vol. VI, No. 2, 1961.

E. Cave, *The Gentleman's Magazine*, Vol. 32, 1762.

James Hadden, *A History of Uniontown: the County Seat of Fayette County*, Pennsylvania, Printed by the New Werner Co., 1913.

Gail Hamilton, *Biography of James G. Blaine*, H. Bill Publishing Company, 1895.

History of Fayette County, Pennsylvania: With Biographical Sketches of Many of its Pioneers and Prominent Men, Franklin Ellis, editor, Historic Book Collection, University of Pittsburgh, 1882.

Jason Jarrell and Sarah Farmer, *Ages of the Giants: a Cultural History of the Tall Ones in Prehistoric America*, Serpent Mound Books and Press, 2017.

Craig M. Klugman, *Dead Men Talking: Evidence of Post Death Contact and Continuing Bonds*, Omega, 2006.

Joseph Élie Méric, *Revue du Monde Invisible*, Vol. 8, 1905-1906.

Thomas B. Searight, *The Old Pike: a History of the National Road, with Incidents, Accidents, and Anecdotes Thereon* Historic Book Collection, University of Pittsburgh, 1894.

James Veech, *The Monongahela of Old: or, Historical Sketches of South-western Pennsylvania to the Year 1800*, Historic Book Collection, University of Pittsburgh, 1910.

Lewis Clark Walkinshaw, *Annals of Southwestern Pennsylvania, Vol. 1*, Lewis Historical Publishing Company, Inc., New York NY, 1939.

ALSO AVAILABLE
FROM
FRIGHTENING FLOYDS
PUBLISHING

MORE
MYSTERIOUS TALES
FROM
ANUBIS PRESS

HAUNTED SURRY TO SUFFOLK:
SPOOKY LOCATIONS ALONG ROUTES 10 AND 460

Take a journey along Virginia's scenic Routes 10 and 460 eastbound to enjoy the lovely countryside and metropolises that spread around these two roads. Most of all, discover that some historical houses, plantations, battlefields, parks, and even the modern cities, have more than touristy knickknacks, ham, and peanuts to offer. Many have ghosts!

Bacon's Castle has spirits haunting it since the 1600s. Stay in a cabin overnight at Chippokes Plantation State Park and you might find you have a spectral bedfellow. The city of Smithfield has more to offer than the world's oldest ham; it also has some very old phantoms still stalking its buildings. Take a ghost tour of Suffolk and see why the biggest little city is also one of the spookiest. Discover the myths and legends of the Great Dismal Swamp and see what phantoms are still haunting the wildlife refuge. And if that's not enough, Bigfoot and UFOs are part of the paranormal scenery. These and other areas of southeastern Virginia are teeming with ghosts, Sasquatch, UFOs, and monsters. See what awaits you along 460 south and 10. No matter which road you take, the phantoms can't wait to SCARE you a good time.

HANDBOOK FOR THE DEAD

DON'T FORGET YOUR HANDBOOK...

Welcome all spirits! The Frightening Floyds present to you, *Handbook for the Dead* – a guide to help all new manifestations realize their functional perimeters.

Within this anthology, you'll read paranormal accounts from individuals who have experienced phantoms and disturbances that have not only chilled them, but also left them with some new insight into the supernatural. Now, they want to share their stories and wisdom with you. That way, if you're feeling a little flat, or even if you're a lost soul, you won't have to draw a door and knock.

Handbook for the Dead is sure to please the strange and unusual in everyone, and we promise it doesn't read like stereo instructions.

ALIENS OVER KENTUCKY

From the Frightening Floyds, the pair of paranormal enthusiasts who brought you *Be Our Ghost* and *Haunts of Hollywood Stars and Starlets* comes a new adventure into the realm of the unknown – *Aliens over Kentucky*.

This collection includes the most noted extraterrestrial encounters from the Bluegrass State, such as the Kelly Creatures Incident of 1955, the Stanford Abductions, the Dogfight above General Electric, and the tale of Capt. Thomas Mantell chasing a UFO through Kentucky skies. But that's not all. There are lesser known, but equally intriguing, reports herein, such as the train collision with the UFO, stories of unexplained crop circles and cattle mutilations, Spring-heeled Jack, the Meat Shower of 1876, and many eyewitness reports of various unidentified crafts. You'll also read a couple of personal experiences from the authors, and even Muhammad Ali gets involved in the alien action.

Join Jacob and Jenny Floyd as they dig into the mysterious cases and theories regarding Kentucky's "X-Files". Just be sure to keep one eye on the book and the other on the sky…

BE OUR GHOST

The Frightening Floyds invite you to be our ghost as we take you on a tour of the happiest haunted place on Earth! In this book, you will read about much of the alleged paranormal activity as well as urban legends spanning the various Disney theme parks around the world. From the haunted dolls of It's a Small World to the real ghosts of the Haunted Mansion, there are many spirits here to greet you. And make sure to say "Good morning" to George at Pirates of the Caribbean.

Enjoy the spooky and fascinating tales in *Be Our Ghost*! And don't worry, there are no hitchhiking ghosts ahead…or are there?

PARANORMAL ENCOUNTERS

The Frightening Floyds present *Paranormal Encounters*: a collection of 14 tales of true ghostly experiences. From a malevolent spirit remaining in an apartment, to a loving phone call from a lost relative; from a house with a sliding chair and slamming doors, to a snow globe moving across a bedroom; from a possible past-life experience to a ghostly stranger in a radio station, this anthology contains several strange and unusual stories that are sure to entertain fans of the paranormal.

HAUNTS OF HOLLYWOOD STARS AND STARLETS

Explore the dark side of Tinseltown in this collection of paranormal stories, conspiracy theories, curses, and legends about some of Hollywood's most iconic names: Marilyn Monroe, Rudolph Valentino, Charlie Chaplin, James Dean, Jean Harlow, Clark and Carole, Lucille Ball, Michael Jackson, Bela Lugosi, Lon Cheney, John Belushi, and the King himself—Elvis Presley—and many more. Join the Frightening Floyds as they take you on a terrifying journey through the city of glamour and glitz!

Available on Amazon in paperback and Kindle!

FOR WESTERN
ADVENTURES
TRY
WILD WEST PRESS

BELLA

In an alternate 1800's America, where magic is real and dragons soar through the skies of the American frontier –

Topher had a good life, mostly. It wasn't great, but what can a young African girl expect living on the Edge of the World!

She had a shack that she shared with her Ma, she knew what vendors she could pocket an apple from, and was better than anyone with a spitshot. What more could a girl in the slums expect?

Then that chucklehead Wasco rolled out of the mountains like a toppled boulder. Topher had figured he might be good for a penny or two if she showed him around. Before she knew it he had her trompin' around the Blacklands, getting shot at, almost eaten and damn near gutted by some bull-headed dandy!

Jacob, who was about the handsomest gunfighter a body could imagine, might be some kind of monster. Old Ying turned out to be one of them wizards from the storybooks and Li had a magic sword!

All because someone went and took Bella and Wasco aimed to get her back, and Topher had been too stubborn not to follow him.

Yeah, it had been a good enough life. She just wasn't sure she was going to make it back to it, or if she even wanted to.

IF YOU LIKE HORROR,
STEP INTO THESE
TALES OF TERROR FROM
NIGHTMARE PRESS

BUTCHERS

Kidnapped, turned, and locked away in a concrete basement, high school student Sey-Mi is taught the ways of the damned. Her captors, beautiful and malignant, cruel and insane, torture her until she pledges allegiance to the *Gwanlyo*, a secret organization of vampires now obsessed with bringing her into their ranks.

Enter Cheol Yu and Hyeri, rogue members who want to liberate vampires and set them upon humankind like a plague. Their first act of rebellion is to persuade Sey-Mi to join them in their twisted objective of unraveling this draconian society of the dead. Before they can do that, they will have to dodge the Natural Police, an order within the *Gwanlyo* whose objective is to hunt down and butcher any vampires that break the organization's strict rules, and who are currently tracking Cheol Yu for murdering one of their own. Hyeri, who is no stranger to the organization's wicked methods of agonizing punishment, is hell-bent on bringing them down, and is prepared to lead Cheol Yu through the dark, abandoned streets of the *Gwanlyo*'s compound where Sey-Mi is being held captive. She doesn't intend to go in unarmed, however. Hyeri has a plan – one that might just burn the *Gwanlyo* to the ground.

Will Sey-Mi place her loyalties in the *Gwanlyo* that rules through terror? Will she side with rebellious conspirators who strive to bring hell to the world? Or will she carve out her own path through the flesh and bone of anyone who stands in her way?

Find out in *Butchers*, a novella of extreme horror.

CHAINSAW SISTERS

When Sis wakes up in her father's backyard, staring at a rickety old shed, she can't remember how she got there or even who she is. But she remembers Amy, the sister that disappeared long ago, the same sister that she now hears calling to her from the shed.

When Sis enters the shed she discovers that Amy is only there in spirit, and she is speaking to her through a new body, and that body just happens to be a chainsaw.

Amy reveals to Sis that she was murdered by a local crime ring and she needs Sis to seek revenge for her. Sis agrees to the task and as Amy guides her to the home of each man responsible, Sis uses Amy's new body to hack them to pieces.

But the situation isn't as straightforward as it seems. As Sis comes face to face with each man, she finds herself in the middle of unfamiliar flashbacks that put her at the scene of a heinous crime of which she has no recollection. In time, she begins to believe that these are not her memories and Amy isn't telling her everything she needs to know.

What lies ahead beyond the coming bloodbath is something darker and more disturbing than Sis could have imagined. Who is Amy? Who is Sis? And what connection do they both have to the men she's about to murder?

And why is her sister now a telepathic chainsaw?

Also includes three short stories about a demonic hollow, killer pizzas, and space zombies.

ANIMAL UPRISING!

A lion, a hybrid, a bear – oh no! A goat, a gull, and a big black dog! Can't forget the roaches, the deer flies, and the tarantula hawk, or the abominable insect that rises from the earth! We got creepy crawlers and killer critters for everyone. Oh, you want mythical creatures? How about a malevolent spirit posed as a fox, a rambunctious jackalope, or a herd of unicorn-gazelles on a distant planet? Let's not forget the supernatural silver stag with the power to raise the dead. Oh, did I mention the giant mantis shrimp? Yeah – we got a giant mantis shrimp. Humankind really has their work cut out for them in this collection of terrifying tales of beastly butchery. Need to know more? Check out *Animal Uprising!* for all of the mayhem.

NIGHT OF THE POSSUMS

JACOB FLOYD

The night of the possums began on a chilly autumn morning around 2am in late October.

On a dark country road, a young man is torn to shreds by wild animals. The news of his grisly death rocks the town. When a similar death occurs later that day, the town is in the grips of fear.

In rural Bardstown, Kentucky, opossums have risen up against the populace. People are being maimed and devoured throughout the city. These are not your ordinary opossums, either: they are smarter, stronger, faster, and far more vicious—some larger than any opossum anyone has ever seen, growing as long as four feet and as heavy as fifty pounds, with teeth capable of cleaving bone.

As the flesh-eating scourge quickly spreads from one end of Bardstown to the other, a few of those who survived the attacks band together in an attempt to eradicate the maniac marsupials. But, the number of the beasts grows by the hour and the force becomes too insurmountable and the survivors soon realize escape is their only option.

But, beyond the berserk behavior of the carnivorous creatures is a darker secret—something ancient and unnatural that threatens all those who are bitten. Before anyone can find out what is driving these opossums to kill, the survivors must battle their way through the merciless onslaught of claws and teeth and leave the threat of Bardstown behind them.

POETRY FANS, CHECK OUT POET TREE GROVE

MAN IN THE SHADOW LAND

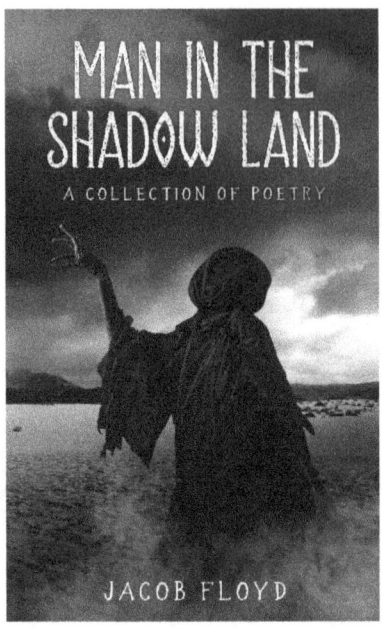

Welcome to the Shadow Land…

In this book, you will find poems about death, sorrow, madness, fear, and other aspects of life that haunt the Man in the Shadow Land. This collection spans ten years of the author's life, and contains some of his most authentic pieces. From his Poe-inspired poetry to those written from the darkest places of his heart, *Man in the Shadow Land* is a journey into a soul full of shadowy corners.

COMING SOON:

FROM ANUBIS PRESS:

Haunted Hotels of Virginia
Susan Schwartz

Kentucky's Strange and Unusual Haunts
The Frightening Floyds

The Frightening Floyds' Big Book of Monsters
The Frightening Floyds

FROM NIGHTMARE PRESS:

Retro Horror
An anthology

The Gray Man of Smoke and Shadows
Todd Sullivan

Jumping Jack Slash
Jacob Floyd

The Cursed Diary of a Brooklyn Dog Walker
Michael Reyes

The Untaken
Bekki Pate

The Possums of Dawn
Jacob Floyd

FROM WILD WEST PRESS

The Dark Frontier
An anthology

Thank you for reading! If you like the book, please leave a review on Amazon and Goodreads. Reviews help authors and publishers spread the word!

To keep up with more Anubis Press news, join the Anubis Press Dynasty on Facebook.

www.ingramcontent.com/pod-product-compliance
Lightning Source LLC
Chambersburg PA
CBHW031556040426
42452CB00006B/318